## U.S. Fish & Wildlife Service

# Adaptive Harvest Management

## *2007 Hunting Season*

$15
VOID AFTER
JUNE 30,
2008

*Ring-
Necked Duck*

U.S. DEPARTMENT OF THE INTERIOR

MIGRATORY BIRD HUNTING AND CONSERVATION STAMP

# Adaptive Harvest Management

## *2007 Hunting Season*

## PREFACE

The process of setting waterfowl hunting regulations is conducted annually in the United States (Blohm 1989). This process involves a number of meetings where the status of waterfowl is reviewed by the agencies responsible for setting hunting regulations. In addition, the U.S. Fish and Wildlife Service (USFWS) publishes proposed regulations in the *Federal Register* to allow public comment. This document is part of a series of reports intended to support development of harvest regulations for the 2007 hunting season. Specifically, this report is intended to provide waterfowl managers and the public with information about the use of adaptive harvest management (AHM) for setting waterfowl hunting regulations in the United States. This report provides the most current data, analyses, and decision-making protocols. However, adaptive management is a dynamic process and some information presented in this report will differ from that in previous reports.

*Citation:* U.S. Fish and Wildlife Service. 2007. Adaptive Harvest Management: 2007 Hunting Season. U.S. Dept. Interior, Washington, D.C. 44pp. Available online at http://www.fws.gov/migratorybirds/mgmt/AHM/AHM-intro htm

## ACKNOWLEDGMENTS

A working group comprised of representatives from the USFWS, the U.S. Geological Survey (USGS), the Canadian Wildlife Service (CWS), and the four Flyway Councils (Appendix A) was established in 1992 to review the scientific basis for managing waterfowl harvests. The working group, supported by technical experts from the waterfowl management and research communities, subsequently proposed a framework for adaptive harvest management, which was first implemented in 1995. The USFWS expresses its gratitude to the AHM Working Group and to the many other individuals, organizations, and agencies that have contributed to the development and implementation of AHM.

This report was prepared by the USFWS Division of Migratory Bird Management. F. A. Johnson and G. S. Boomer were the principal authors. Individuals that provided essential information or otherwise assisted with report preparation were P. Garrettson (USFWS), T. Liddick (USGS), M. Otto (USFWS), R. Raftovich (USFWS), A. Royle (USGS), M. Runge (USGS), T. Sanders (USFWS), and K. Wilkins (USFWS). Comments regarding this document should be sent to the Chief, Division of Migratory Bird Management - USFWS, 4401 North Fairfax Drive, MS MSP-4107, Arlington, VA 22203.

# TABLE OF CONTENTS

# EXECUTIVE SUMMARY

In 1995 the U.S. Fish and Wildlife Service (USFWS) implemented the Adaptive Harvest Management (AHM) program for setting duck hunting regulations in the United States. The AHM approach provides a framework for making objective decisions in the face of incomplete knowledge concerning waterfowl population dynamics and regulatory impacts.

The current AHM protocol is based on the population dynamics and status of two mallard (*Anas platyrhynchos*) stocks. Mid-continent mallards are defined as those breeding in the so-called traditional survey area, plus the states of Michigan, Minnesota, and Wisconsin. The prescribed regulatory alternative for the Mississippi, Central, and Pacific Flyways depends exclusively on the status of these mallards. Eastern mallards are defined as those breeding in the states of Virginia northward into Vermont, and in survey strata located on the Canadian side of the St. Lawrence River. The regulatory choice for the Atlantic Flyway depends exclusively on the status of these mallards. Investigations of the population dynamics of western mallards and their potential effect on hunting regulations in the West are on-going.

Mallard population models account for an apparent positive bias in estimates of survival and reproductive rates, and also allow for alternative hypotheses concerning the effects of harvest and the environment in regulating population size. Model-specific weights reflect the relative confidence in alternative hypotheses, and are updated annually using comparisons of predicted and observed population sizes. For mid-continent mallards, current model weights favor the weakly density-dependent reproductive hypothesis (90%). Evidence for the additive-mortality hypothesis remains equivocal (60%). For eastern mallards, virtually all of the weight is on models that have corrections for bias in estimates of survival or reproductive rates. Model weights also favor the strongly density-dependent reproductive hypothesis (59%). By consensus, hunting mortality is assumed to be additive in eastern mallards.

For the 2007 hunting season, the USFWS is considering the same regulatory alternatives as last year. The nature of the restrictive, moderate, and liberal alternatives has remained essentially unchanged since 1997, except that extended framework dates have been offered in the moderate and liberal alternatives since 2002. Harvest rates associated with each of the regulatory alternatives have been updated based on band-reporting rate studies conducted since 1998. Estimated harvest rates of adult males from the 2002-2006 liberal hunting seasons have averaged 0.113 (SE = 0.001) and 0.136 (SE = 0.010) for mid-continent and eastern mallards, respectively. The estimated marginal effect of framework-date extensions has been an increase in harvest rate of 0.009 (SD = 0.008) and 0.005 (SD = 0.010) for mid-continent and eastern mallards, respectively.

Optimal regulatory strategies for the 2007 hunting season were calculated using: (1) harvest-management objectives specific to each mallard stock; (2) the 2007 regulatory alternatives; and (3) current population models and associated weights for mid-continent and eastern mallards. Based on this year's survey results of 9.05 million mid-continent mallards, 5.04 million ponds in Prairie Canada, and 907 thousand eastern mallards, the optimal choice for all four Flyways is the liberal regulatory alternative.

AHM concepts and tools are also being applied to help improve harvest management for several other waterfowl stocks. In the last year, significant progress has been made in understanding the harvest potential of American black ducks (*Anas rubripes*), the Atlantic Population of Canada geese (*Branta canadensis*), northern pintails (*Anas acuta*), and scaup (*Aythya affinis*, *A. marila*). While these biological assessments are on-going, they are already proving valuable in helping focus debate on the social aspects of harvesting policy, including management objectives and the nature of regulatory alternatives.

# BACKGROUND

The annual process of setting duck-hunting regulations in the United States is based on a system of resource monitoring, data analyses, and rule-making (Blohm 1989). Each year, monitoring activities such as aerial surveys and hunter questionnaires provide information on population size, habitat conditions, and harvest levels. Data collected from this monitoring program are analyzed each year, and proposals for duck-hunting regulations are developed by the Flyway Councils, States, and USFWS. After extensive public review, the USFWS announces regulatory guidelines within which States can set their hunting seasons.

In 1995, the USFWS adopted the concept of adaptive resource management (Walters 1986) for regulating duck harvests in the United States. This approach explicitly recognizes that the consequences of hunting regulations cannot be predicted with certainty, and provides a framework for making objective decisions in the face of that uncertainty (Williams and Johnson 1995). Inherent in the adaptive approach is an awareness that management performance can be maximized only if regulatory effects can be predicted reliably. Thus, adaptive management relies on an iterative cycle of monitoring, assessment, and decision-making to clarify the relationships among hunting regulations, harvests, and waterfowl abundance.

In regulating waterfowl harvests, managers face four fundamental sources of uncertainty (Nichols et al. 1995, Johnson et al. 1996, Williams et al. 1996):

(1)   environmental variation - the temporal and spatial variation in weather conditions and other key features of waterfowl habitat; an example is the annual change in the number of ponds in the Prairie Pothole Region, where water conditions influence duck reproductive success;

(2)   partial controllability - the ability of managers to control harvest only within limits; the harvest resulting from a particular set of hunting regulations cannot be predicted with certainty because of variation in weather conditions, timing of migration, hunter effort, and other factors;

(3)   partial observability - the ability to estimate key population attributes (e.g., population size, reproductive rate, harvest) only within the precision afforded by extant monitoring programs; and

(4)   structural uncertainty - an incomplete understanding of biological processes; a familiar example is the long-standing debate about whether harvest is additive to other sources of mortality or whether populations compensate for hunting losses through reduced natural mortality. Structural uncertainty increases contentiousness in the decision-making process and decreases the extent to which managers can meet long-term conservation goals.

AHM was developed as a systematic process for dealing objectively with these uncertainties. The key components of AHM include (Johnson et al. 1993, Williams and Johnson 1995):

(1)   a limited number of regulatory alternatives, which describe Flyway-specific season lengths, bag limits, and framework dates;

(2)   a set of population models describing various hypotheses about the effects of harvest and environmental factors on waterfowl abundance;

(3)   a measure of reliability (probability or "weight") for each population model; and

(4)   a mathematical description of the objective(s) of harvest management (i.e., an "objective function"), by which alternative regulatory strategies can be compared.

These components are used in a stochastic optimization procedure to derive a regulatory strategy. A regulatory strategy specifies the optimal regulatory choice, with respect to the stated management objectives, for each possible combination of breeding population size, environmental conditions, and model weights (Johnson et al. 1997). The setting of annual hunting regulations then involves an iterative process:

(1)   each year, an optimal regulatory choice is identified based on resource and environmental conditions, and on current model weights;

4

(2)     after the regulatory decision is made, model-specific predictions for subsequent breeding population size are determined;

(3)     when monitoring data become available, model weights are increased to the extent that observations of population size agree with predictions, and decreased to the extent that they disagree; and

(4)     the new model weights are used to start another iteration of the process.

By iteratively updating model weights and optimizing regulatory choices, the process should eventually identify which model is the best overall predictor of changes in population abundance. The process is optimal in the sense that it provides the regulatory choice each year necessary to maximize management performance. It is adaptive in the sense that the harvest strategy "evolves" to account for new knowledge generated by a comparison of predicted and observed population sizes.

# MALLARD STOCKS AND FLYWAY MANAGEMENT

Since its inception AHM has focused on the population dynamics and harvest potential of mallards, especially those breeding in mid-continent North America. Mallards constitute a large portion of the total U.S. duck harvest, and traditionally have been a reliable indicator of the status of many other species. As management capabilities have grown, there has been increasing interest in the ecology and management of breeding mallards that occur outside the mid-continent region. Geographic differences in the reproduction, mortality, and migrations of mallard stocks suggest that there may be corresponding differences in optimal levels of sport harvest. The ability to regulate harvests of mallards originating from various breeding areas is complicated, however, by the fact that a large degree of mixing occurs during the hunting season. The challenge for managers, then, is to vary hunting regulations among Flyways in a manner that recognizes each Flyway's unique breeding-ground derivation of mallards. Of course, no Flyway receives mallards exclusively from one breeding area, and so Flyway-specific harvest strategies ideally must account for multiple breeding stocks that are exposed to a common harvest.

The optimization procedures used in AHM can account for breeding populations of mallards beyond the mid-continent region, and for the manner in which these ducks distribute themselves among the Flyways during the hunting season. An optimal approach would allow for Flyway-specific regulatory strategies, which in a sense represent for each Flyway an average of the optimal harvest strategies for each contributing breeding stock, weighted by the relative size of each stock in the fall flight. This joint optimization of multiple mallard stocks requires: (1) models of population dynamics for all recognized stocks of mallards; (2) an objective function that accounts for harvest-management goals for all mallard stocks in the aggregate; and (3) decision rules allowing Flyway-specific regulatory choices.

Currently, two stocks of mallards are officially recognized for the purposes of AHM (Fig. 1). We continue to use a constrained approach to the optimization of these stocks' harvest, in which the Atlantic Flyway regulatory strategy is based exclusively on the status of eastern mallards, and the regulatory strategy for the remaining Flyways is based exclusively on the status of mid-continent mallards. This approach has been determined to perform nearly as well as a joint-optimization because mixing of the two stocks during the hunting season is limited.

Fig 1. Survey areas currently assigned to the mid-continent and eastern stocks of mallards for the purposes of AHM. Delineation of the western-mallard stock is pending further development and review of population models and monitoring programs.

# MALLARD POPULATION DYNAMICS

## Mid-Continent Stock

Mid-continent mallards are defined as those breeding in federal survey strata 1-18, 20-50, and 75-77 (i.e., the "traditional" survey area), and in Minnesota, Wisconsin, and Michigan (Fig. 1). Estimates of the size of this population are available since 1992, and have varied from 6.6 to 11.8 million (Table 1, Fig. 2). Estimated breeding-population size in 2007 was 9.053 (SE = 0.291 million), including 8.307 million (SE = 0.285 million) from the traditional survey area and 746 thousand (SE = 56 thousand) from the Great Lakes region.

Details concerning the set of population models for mid-continent mallards are provided in Appendix B. The set consists of four alternatives, formed by the combination of two survival hypotheses (additive vs. compensatory hunting mortality) and two reproductive hypotheses (strongly vs. weakly density dependent). Relative weights for the alternative models of mid-continent mallards changed little until all models under-predicted the change in population size from 1998 to 1999, perhaps indicating there is a significant factor affecting population dynamics that is absent from all four models (Fig. 3). Updated model weights suggest some preference for the additive-mortality models (60%) over those describing hunting mortality as compensatory (40%). For most of the time frame, model weights have strongly favored the weakly density-dependent reproductive models over the strongly density-dependent ones, with current model weights of 90% and 10%, respectively. The reader is cautioned, however, that models can sometimes make reliable predictions of population size for reasons having little to do with the biological hypotheses expressed therein (Johnson et al. 2002b).

Table 1. Estimates (N) and standard errors (SE) of mallards (in millions) in spring in the traditional survey area (strata 1-18, 20-50, and 75-77) and the states of Minnesota, Wisconsin, and Michigan.

| Year | Traditional survey area | | Great Lakes region | | Total | |
|------|------|--------|------|--------|---------|--------|
|      | N | SE | N | SE | N | SE |
| 1992 | 5.9761 | 0.2410 | 0.9946 | 0.1597 | 6.9706 | 0.2891 |
| 1993 | 5.7083 | 0.2089 | 0.9347 | 0.1457 | 6.6430 | 0.2547 |
| 1994 | 6.9801 | 0.2828 | 1.1505 | 0.1163 | 8.1306 | 0.3058 |
| 1995 | 8.2694 | 0.2875 | 1.1214 | 0.1965 | 9.3908 | 0.3482 |
| 1996 | 7.9413 | 0.2629 | 1.0251 | 0.1443 | 8.9664 | 0.2999 |
| 1997 | 9.9397 | 0.3085 | 1.0777 | 0.1445 | 11.0174 | 0.3407 |
| 1998 | 9.6404 | 0.3016 | 1.1224 | 0.1792 | 10.7628 | 0.3508 |
| 1999 | 10.8057 | 0.3445 | 1.0591 | 0.2122 | 11.8648 | 0.4046 |
| 2000 | 9.4702 | 0.2902 | 1.2350 | 0.1761 | 10.7052 | 0.3395 |
| 2001 | 7.9040 | 0.2269 | 0.8622 | 0.1086 | 8.7662 | 0.2516 |
| 2002 | 7.5037 | 0.2465 | 1.0820 | 0.1152 | 8.5857 | 0.2721 |
| 2003 | 7.9497 | 0.2673 | 0.8360 | 0.0734 | 8.7857 | 0.2772 |
| 2004 | 7.4253 | 0.2820 | 0.9333 | 0.0748 | 8.3586 | 0.2917 |
| 2005 | 6.7553 | 0.2808 | 0.7862 | 0.0650 | 7.5415 | 0.2883 |
| 2006 | 7.2765 | 0.2237 | 0.5881 | 0.0465 | 7.8646 | 0.2284 |
| 2007 | 8.3073 | 0.2858 | 0.7459 | 0.0565 | 9.0532 | 0.2913 |

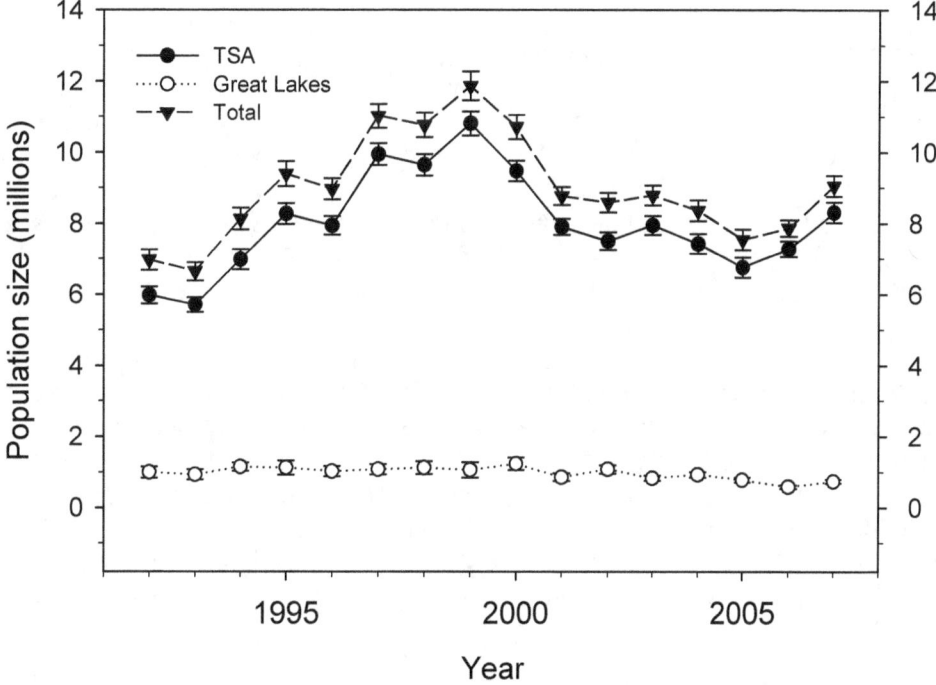

Fig. 2. Population estimates of mid-continent mallards in the traditional survey area (TSA) and the Great Lakes region. Error bars represent one standard error.

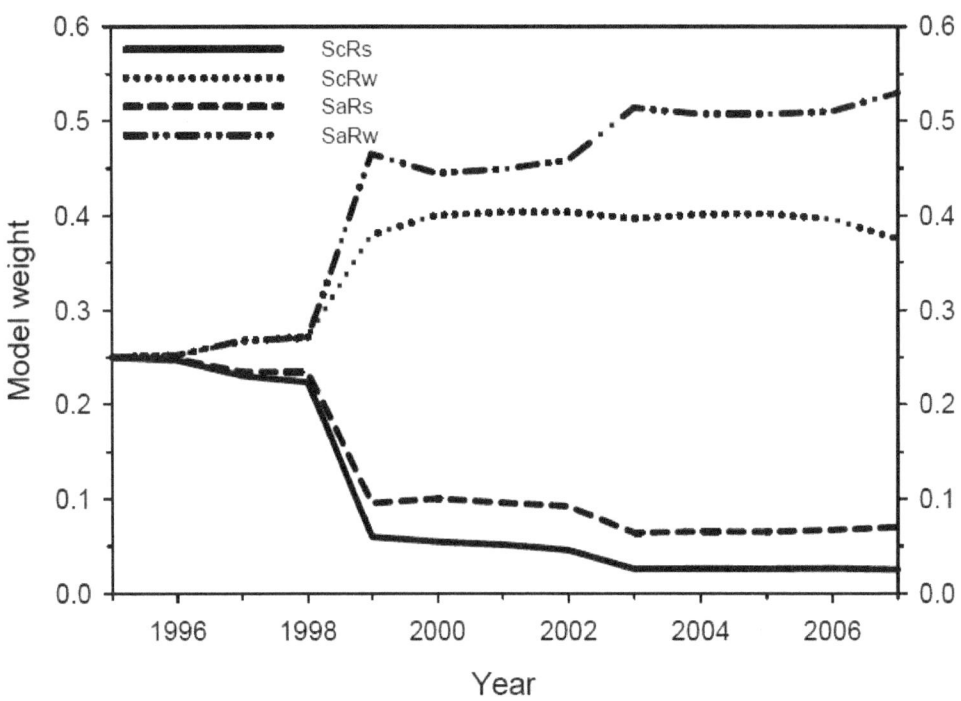

Fig 3. Weights for models of mid-continent mallards (ScRs = compensatory mortality and strongly density-dependent reproduction, ScRw = compensatory mortality and weakly density-dependent reproduction, SaRs = additive mortality and strongly density-dependent reproduction, and SaRw = additive mortality and weakly density-dependent reproduction). Model weights were assumed to be equal in 1995.

## Eastern Stock

Eastern mallards are defined as those breeding in southern Ontario and Quebec (federal survey strata 51-54 and 56) and in the northeastern U.S. (state plot surveys; Heusman and Sauer 2000) (Fig. 1). Estimates of population size have varied from 856 thousand to 1.1 million since 1990, with the majority of the population accounted for in the northeastern U.S. (Table 3, Fig. 4). For 2007, the estimated breeding-population size of eastern mallards was 907 thousand (SE = 58 thousand), including 688 thousand (SE = 47 thousand) from the northeastern U.S. and 219 thousand (SE = 34 thousand) from the Canadian survey strata. The reader is cautioned that these estimates differ from those reported in the USFWS annual waterfowl trend and status reports, which include composite estimates based on more fixed-wing strata in eastern Canada and helicopter surveys conducted by CWS.

Details concerning the set of population models for eastern mallards are provided in Appendix C. The set consists of six alternatives, formed by the combination of two reproductive hypotheses (strongly vs. weakly density dependent) and three hypotheses concerning bias in estimates of survival and reproductive rates (no bias vs. biased survival rates vs. biased reproductive rates). With respect to model weights, there is no single model that is clearly favored over the others at the current time. Collectively, the models with strong density-dependent reproduction are slightly better predictors of changes in population size than those with weak density dependence, with current model weights of 59% and 41%, respectively (Fig. 5). In addition, there is overwhelming evidence of bias in extant estimates of survival or reproductive rates (100%), assuming that survey estimates are unbiased.

Table 3. Estimates (N) and associated standard errors (SE) of mallards (in thousands) in spring in the northeastern U.S. (state plot surveys) and eastern Canada (federal survey strata 51-54 and 56).

| | Northeastern U.S. | | Canadian survey strata | | Total | |
|---|---|---|---|---|---|---|
| Year | N | SE | N | SE | N | SE |
| 1990 | 665.1 | 78.3 | 190.7 | 47.2 | 855.8 | 91.4 |
| 1991 | 779.2 | 88.3 | 152.8 | 33.7 | 932.0 | 94.5 |
| 1992 | 562.2 | 47.9 | 320.3 | 53.0 | 882.5 | 71.5 |
| 1993 | 683.1 | 49.7 | 292.1 | 48.2 | 975.2 | 69.3 |
| 1994 | 853.1 | 62.7 | 219.5 | 28.2 | 1072.5 | 68.7 |
| 1995 | 862.8 | 70.2 | 184.4 | 40.0 | 1047.2 | 80.9 |
| 1996 | 848.4 | 61.1 | 283.1 | 55.7 | 1131.5 | 82.6 |
| 1997 | 795.1 | 49.6 | 212.1 | 39.6 | 1007.2 | 63.4 |
| 1998 | 775.1 | 49.7 | 263.8 | 67.2 | 1038.9 | 83.6 |
| 1999 | 879.7 | 60.2 | 212.5 | 36.9 | 1092.2 | 70.6 |
| 2000 | 757.8 | 48.5 | 132.3 | 26.4 | 890.0 | 55.2 |
| 2001 | 807.5 | 51.4 | 200.2 | 35.6 | 1007.7 | 62.5 |
| 2002 | 834.1 | 56.2 | 171.3 | 30.0 | 1005.4 | 63.8 |
| 2003 | 731.8 | 47.0 | 308.3 | 55.4 | 1040.1 | 72.6 |
| 2004 | 809.1 | 51.8 | 301.5 | 53.3 | 1110.7 | 74.3 |
| 2005 | 753.6 | 53.6 | 293.4 | 53.1 | 1047.0 | 75.5 |
| 2006 | 725.2 | 47.9 | 174.0 | 28.4 | 899.2 | 55.7 |
| 2007 | 687.6 | 46.7 | 219.3 | 33.6 | 906.9 | 57.6 |

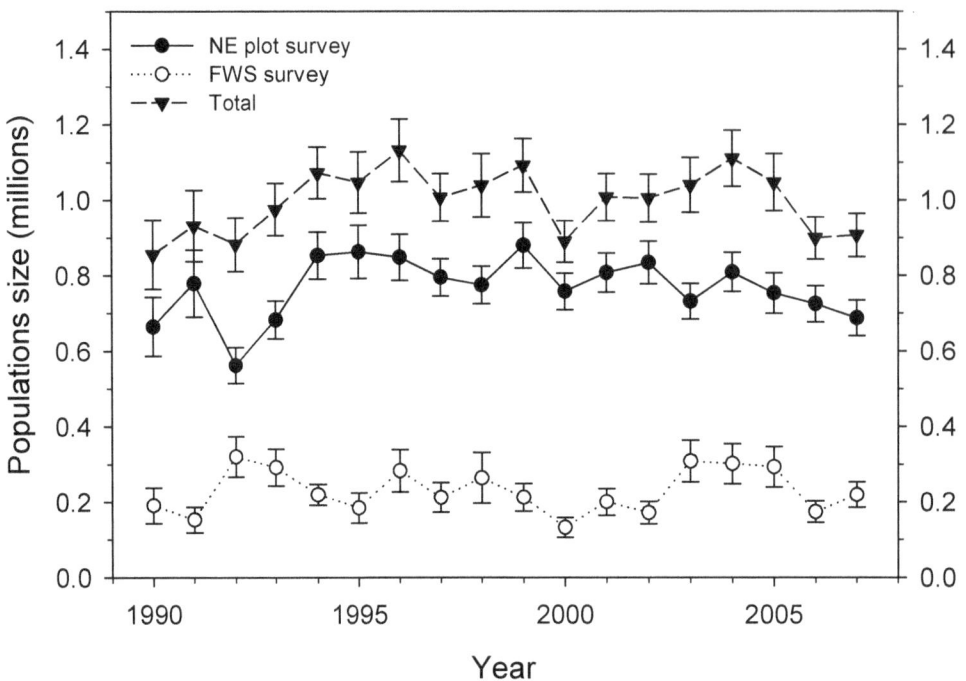

Fig. 4. Population estimates of eastern mallards in the northeastern U.S. (NE plot survey) and in federal surveys in southern Ontario and Quebec (FWS survey). Error bars represent one standard error.

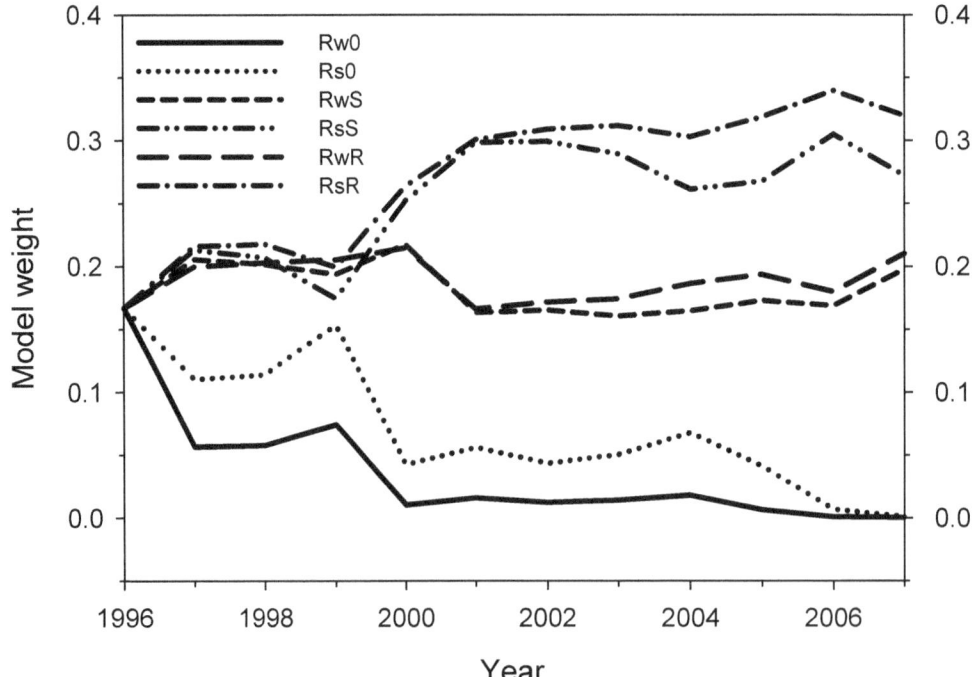

Fig. 5. Weights for models of eastern mallards (Rw0 = weak density-dependent reproduction and no model bias, Rs0 = strong -dependent reproduction and no model bias, RwS = weak density-dependent reproduction and biased survival rates, RsS = strong density-dependent reproduction and biased survival rates, RwR = weak density-dependent reproduction and biased reproductive ates, and RsR = strong density-dependent reproduction and biased reproductive rates). Model weights were assumed to be equal in 1996.

# Western Stock

Recent efforts to develop Flyway-specific harvest strategies have focused on mallards breeding in the states of the Pacific Flyway (including Alaska), British Columbia, and the Yukon Territory. Efforts to understand and model the population dynamics of western mallards have been underway for several years and the Pacific Flyway States, the USFWS, and the Canadian Wildlife Service have been collaborating to improve survey and banding programs. We summarize the most recent results concerning the dynamics of these mallards, as well as some implications for harvest management. A more detailed report is available on-line at http://www.fws.gov/migratorybirds/mgmt/ahm/special-topics.htm.

Western mallards are distributed over a large area and we have had continuing concerns about our ability to determine changes in population size based on the collection of surveys conducted independently by Pacific Flyway States and the Province of British Columbia. These surveys tend to vary in design and intensity, and in some cases lack measures of precision. Therefore, we reviewed extant surveys to determine their adequacy for supporting a western-mallard AHM protocol and ultimately selected Alaska, California, and Oregon for modeling purposes. These three states likely harbor about 75% of the western-mallard breeding population. Nonetheless, this geographic delineation is considered temporary until surveys in other areas can be brought up to similar standards and an adequate record of population estimates is available for analysis.

To predict changes in abundance we relied on a discrete logistic model, which combines reproduction and natural mortality into a single parameter $r$, the intrinsic rate of growth. This model assumes density-dependent growth, which is regulated by the ratio of population size, $N$, to the carrying capacity of the environment, $K$ (i.e., population size in the absence of harvest). In the traditional formulation of the logistic model, harvest mortality is completely additive and any compensation for hunting losses occurs as a result of density-dependent responses beginning in the subsequent breeding season. To increase the model's generality we included a scaling parameter for harvest that allows for the possibility of compensation prior to the breeding season. It is important to note, however, that this parameterization does not incorporate any hypothesized mechanism for harvest compensation and, therefore, must be interpreted cautiously. We modeled Alaska mallards independently of those in California and Oregon because of differing population trajectories (Fig. 6) and substantial differences in the distribution of band recoveries.

We used Bayesian estimation methods in combination with a state-space model that accounts explicitly for both process and observation error in breeding population size (Meyer and Millar 1999). Breeding population estimates of mallards in Alaska are available since 1955, but we had to limit the time-series to 1990-2005 because of changes in survey methodology and insufficient band-recovery data. The logistic model and associated posterior parameter estimates provided a reasonable fit to the observed time-series of Alaska population estimates. The estimated carrying capacity was 1.2 million, the intrinsic rate of growth was 0.31, and harvest mortality acted in an additive fashion. Breeding population and harvest-rate data were available for California-Oregon mallards for the period 1992-2006. The logistic model also provided a reasonable fit to these data, suggesting a carrying capacity of 0.7 million, an intrinsic rate of growth 0.34, and harvest mortality that acted in only a partially additive manner.

For the purpose of understanding general patterns in optimal harvest rates, we assumed perfect control over harvest and evaluated state-dependent harvest rates from 0.0 to 0.25 in increments of 0.05. We examined two different management objectives conditioned on this set of harvest rates: (1) maximize long-term cumulative yield; and (2) attain approximately 90% of the maximum long-term cumulative yield. For an objective to maximize long-term cumulative harvest, there were many combinations of stock sizes that had harvest-rate prescriptions of either 0 or 25 percent. Very few stock sizes had intermediate harvest-rate prescriptions. In contrast, an objective to attain 90% of the maximum yield produced an optimal strategy with a more even distribution of optimal harvest rates, and very few prescriptions for closed seasons.

Empirical estimates of harvest rates showed no obvious response to changes in regulations, based on extensive

11

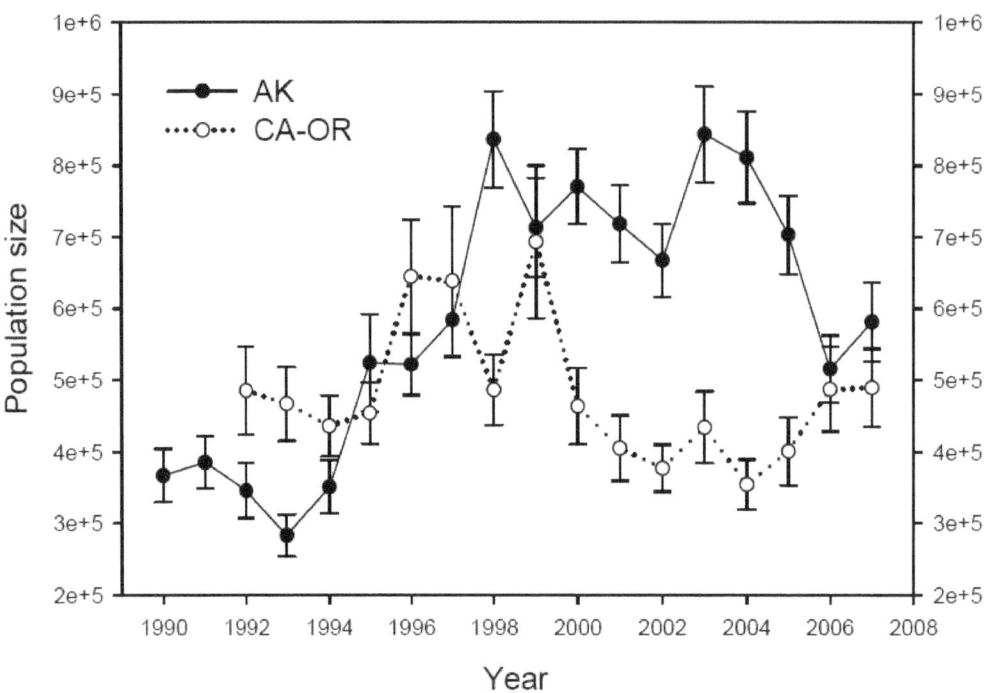

Fig. 6. Estimated abundances of mallards breeding in Alaska and California-Oregon as derived from federal and state surveys, respectively. Error bars represent one standard error.

analyses using a variety of regulatory metrics, including season length, mallard bag limits, and framework opening and closing dates (singly and in combination). We were forced to conclude that changes in regulations in the Pacific Flyway since 1980 have not resulted in significant changes in the harvest rates of western mallards. It appears that more extreme regulatory changes than those used in the past may be needed to effect substantive changes in harvest rates. To help understand the implications of this apparent lack of control over harvest rates, we assumed the most extreme case of two regulatory options: a closed season and an open season. We assumed that an open season would produce a harvest rate of 0.1259 (the mean of all our estimates) and that a closed season would produce a harvest rate of 0.0. We then conducted an optimization to determine the population thresholds for season closures assuming minimal control over harvest rates. Generally, as long as both stocks are above about 350k, then the optimal choice is an open season. Below that, the lower one stock is, the higher the other has to be to maintain an open season.

We believe that the models developed thus far provide a sufficient basis for developing an initial AHM protocol. Moreover, extant monitoring of mallard abundance and harvest rates in Alaska and California-Oregon will provide the necessary basis for updating estimates of model parameters and their variances. Similarly, we believe that sufficient information is available to inform the choice of an objective function for western mallards. For example, an objective to attain 90% of the maximum long-term cumulative harvest provides for levels of hunting opportunity that are similar to those now in effect for a wide range of stock sizes. On a more pessimistic note, we were unable to establish a viable set of regulatory alternatives with which to effect changes in harvest rate. Therefore, an essential task is consideration of hunting regulations beyond the realm of experience that might be expected to have a meaningful effect on harvest rates.

Ideally, the development of AHM protocols for mallards would consider how different breeding stocks distribute themselves among the four flyways so that Flyway-specific harvest strategies could account for the mixing of birds during the hunting season. At present, however, a joint optimization of western, mid-continent, and eastern stocks is not feasible due to computational hurdles. Therefore, the initial AHM protocol for western mallards may need to be structured similarly to that used for eastern mallards, in which an optimal harvest strategy is based on

12

the status of a single breeding stock and harvest regulations in a single flyway. Although the contribution of mid-continent mallards to the Pacific Flyway harvest is significant, we believe an independent harvest strategy for western mallards poses little risk to the mid-continent stock. Further analyses will be needed to confirm this conclusion, as well as to better understand the potential effect of mid-continent mallard status on sustainable hunting opportunities in the Pacific Flyway.

# HARVEST-MANAGEMENT OBJECTIVES

The basic harvest-management objective for mid-continent mallards is to maximize cumulative harvest over the long term, which inherently requires perpetuation of a viable population. Moreover, this objective is constrained to avoid regulations that could be expected to result in a subsequent population size below the goal of the North American Waterfowl Management Plan (NAWMP). According to this constraint, the value of harvest decreases proportionally as the difference between the goal and expected population size increases. This balance of harvest and population objectives results in a regulatory strategy that is more conservative than that for maximizing long-term harvest, but more liberal than a strategy to attain the NAWMP goal (regardless of effects on hunting opportunity). The current objective uses a population goal of 8.8 million mallards, which is based on 8.2 million mallards in the traditional survey area (from the 1998 update of the NAWMP) and a goal of 0.6 million for the combined states of Minnesota, Wisconsin, and Michigan.

For eastern mallards, there is no NAWMP goal or other established target for desired population size. Accordingly, the management objective for eastern mallards is simply to maximize long-term cumulative (i.e., sustainable) harvest.

# REGULATORY ALTERNATIVES

## Evolution of Alternatives

When AHM was first implemented in 1995, three regulatory alternatives characterized as liberal, moderate, and restrictive were defined based on regulations used during 1979-84, 1985-87, and 1988-93, respectively. These regulatory alternatives also were considered for the 1996 hunting season. In 1997, the regulatory alternatives were modified to include: (1) the addition of a very-restrictive alternative; (2) additional days and a higher duck bag limit in the moderate and liberal alternatives; and (3) an increase in the bag limit of hen mallards in the moderate and liberal alternatives. In 2002 the USFWS further modified the moderate and liberal alternatives to include extensions of approximately one week in both the opening and closing framework dates.

In 2003 the very-restrictive alternative was eliminated at the request of the Flyway Councils. Expected harvest rates under the very-restrictive alternative did not differ significantly from those under the restrictive alternative, and the very-restrictive alternative was expected to be prescribed for <5% of all hunting seasons. Also, at the request of the Flyway Councils the USFWS agreed to exclude closed duck-hunting seasons from the AHM protocol when the population size of mid-continent mallards is ≥5.5 million (traditional survey area plus the Great Lakes region). Based on our assessment, closed hunting seasons do not appear to be necessary from the perspective of sustainable harvesting when the mid-continent mallard population exceeds this level. The impact of maintaining open seasons above this level also appears to be negligible for other mid-continent duck species, as based on population models developed by Johnson (2003). However, complete or partial season-closures for particular species or populations could still be deemed necessary in some situations regardless of the status of mid-continent mallards. Details of the regulatory alternatives for each Flyway are provided in Table 6.

Table 6. Regulatory alternatives for the 2007 duck-hunting season.

| | Flyway | | | |
|---|---|---|---|---|
| Regulation | Atlantic[a] | Mississippi | Central[b] | Pacific[c] |
| Shooting hours | one-half hour before sunrise to sunset | | | |
| Framework dates | | | | |
| Restrictive | Oct 1 - Jan 20 | Saturday nearest Oct 1to the Sunday nearest Jan 20 | | |
| Moderate and Liberal | Saturday nearest September 24 to the last Sunday in January | | | |
| Season length (days) | | | | |
| Restrictive | 30 | 30 | 39 | 60 |
| Moderate | 45 | 45 | 60 | 86 |
| Liberal | 60 | 60 | 74 | 107 |
| Bag limit (total / mallard / female mallard) | | | | |
| Restrictive | 3 / 3 / 1 | 3 / 2 / 1 | 3 / 3 / 1 | 4 / 3 / 1 |
| Moderate | 6 / 4 / 2 | 6 / 4 / 1 | 6 / 5 / 1 | 7 / 5 / 2 |
| Liberal | 6 / 4 / 2 | 6 / 4 / 2 | 6 / 5 / 2 | 7 / 7 / 2 |

[a] The states of Maine, Massachusetts, Connecticut, Pennsylvania, New Jersey, Maryland, Delaware, West Virginia, Virginia, and North Carolina are permitted to exclude Sundays, which are closed to hunting, from their total allotment of season days.
[b] The High Plains Mallard Management Unit is allowed 8, 12, and 23 extra days in the restrictive, moderate, and liberal alternatives, respectively.
[c] The Columbia Basin Mallard Management Unit is allowed seven extra days in the restrictive, and moderate alternatives.

# Regulation-Specific Harvest Rates

Harvest rates of mallards associated with each of the open-season regulatory alternatives were initially predicted using harvest-rate estimates from 1979-84, which were adjusted to reflect current hunter numbers and contemporary specifications of season lengths and bag limits. In the case of closed seasons in the U.S., we assumed rates of harvest would be similar to those observed in Canada during 1988-93, which was a period of restrictive regulations both in Canada and the U.S. All harvest-rate predictions were based only in part on band-recovery data, and relied heavily on models of hunting effort and success derived from hunter surveys (USFWS 2002: Appendix C). As such, these predictions had large sampling variances and their accuracy was uncertain.

In 2002 we began relying on Bayesian statistical methods for improving regulation-specific predictions of harvest rates, including predictions of the effects of framework-date extensions. Essentially, the idea is to use existing (prior) information to develop initial harvest-rate predictions (as above), to make regulatory decisions based on those predictions, and then to observe realized harvest rates. Those observed harvest rates, in turn, are treated as new sources of information for calculating updated (posterior) predictions. Bayesian methods are attractive because they provide a quantitative and formal, yet intuitive, approach to adaptive management.

For mid-continent mallards, we have empirical estimates of harvest rate from the recent period of liberal hunting regulations (1998-2006). The Bayesian methods thus allow us to combine these estimates with our prior predictions to provide updated estimates of harvest rates expected under the liberal regulatory alternative. Moreover, in the absence of experience (so far) with the restrictive and moderate regulatory alternatives, we reasoned that our initial predictions of harvest rates associated with those alternatives should be re-scaled based on a comparison of predicted and observed harvest rates under the liberal regulatory alternative. In other words, if observed harvest rates under the liberal alternative were 10% less than predicted, then we might also expect that the mean harvest rate under the moderate alternative would be 10% less than predicted. The appropriate scaling factors currently are based exclusively on prior beliefs about differences in mean harvest rate among regulatory alternatives, but they will be updated once we have experience with something other than the liberal alternative. A detailed description of the analytical framework for modeling mallard harvest rates is provided in Appendix D.

Our models of regulation-specific harvest rates also allow for the marginal effect of framework-date extensions in the moderate and liberal alternatives. A previous analysis by the USFWS (2001) suggested that implementation of framework-date extensions might be expected to increase the harvest rate of mid-continent mallards by about 15%, or in absolute terms by about 0.02 (SD = 0.01). Based on the observed harvest rates during the 2002-2006 hunting seasons, the updated (posterior) estimate of the marginal change in harvest rate attributable to the framework-date extension is 0.009 (SD = 0.008). The estimated effect of the framework-date extension has been to increase harvest rate of mid-continent mallards by about 8% over what would otherwise be expected in the liberal alternative. However, the reader is strongly cautioned that reliable inference about the marginal effect of framework-date extensions ultimately depends on a rigorous experimental design (including controls and random application of treatments).

Current predictions of harvest rates of adult-male mid-continent mallards associated with each of the regulatory alternatives are provided in Table 7. Predictions of harvest rates for the other age-sex cohorts are based on the historical ratios of cohort-specific harvest rates to adult-male rates (Runge et al. 2002). These ratios are considered fixed at their long-term averages and are 1.5407, 0.7191, and 1.1175 for young males, adult females, and young females, respectively. We continued to make the simplifying assumption that the harvest rates of mid-continent mallards depend solely on the regulatory choice in the western three Flyways. This appears to be a reasonable assumption given the small proportion of mid-continent mallards wintering in the Atlantic Flyway (Munro and Kimball 1982), and harvest-rate predictions that suggest a minimal effect of Atlantic Flyway regulations (USFWS 2000). Under this assumption, the optimal regulatory strategy for the western three Flyways can be derived by ignoring the harvest regulations imposed in the Atlantic Flyway.

Table 7. Predictions of harvest rates of adult-male mid-continent mallards expected with application of the 2007 regulatory alternatives in the three western Flyways.

| Regulatory alternative | Mean | SD |
| --- | --- | --- |
| Closed (U.S.) | 0.0088 | 0.0019 |
| Restrictive | 0.0578 | 0.0129 |
| Moderate | 0.1059 | 0.0216 |
| Liberal | 0.1225 | 0.0205 |

The predicted harvest rates of eastern-mallard are updated in the same fashion as that for mid-continent mallards based on reward banding conducted in eastern Canada and the northeastern U.S. (Appendix D). Like mid-continent mallards, harvest rates of age and sex cohorts other than adult male mallards are based on constant rates of differential vulnerability as derived from band-recovery data. For eastern mallards, these constants are 1.153, 1.331, and 1.509 for adult females, young males, and young females, respectively (Johnson et al. 2002a). Regulation-specific predictions of harvest rates of adult-male eastern mallards are provided in Table 8.

In contrast to mid-continent mallards, framework-date extensions were expected to increase the harvest rate of eastern mallards by only about 5% (USFWS 2001), or in absolute terms by about 0.01 (SD = 0.01). Based on the observed harvest rates during the 2002-2006 hunting seasons, the updated (posterior) estimate of the marginal change in harvest rate attributable to the framework-date extension is 0.005 (SD = 0.010). The estimated effect of the framework-date extension has been to increase harvest rate of eastern mallards by about 3% over what would otherwise be expected in the liberal alternative.

Table 8. Predictions of harvest rates of adult-male eastern mallards expected with application of the 2007 regulatory alternatives in the Atlantic Flyway.

| Regulatory alternative | Mean | SD |
|---|---|---|
| Closed (U.S.) | 0.0798 | 0.0233 |
| Restrictive | 0.1202 | 0.0395 |
| Moderate | 0.1471 | 0.0474 |
| Liberal | 0.1578 | 0.0459 |

# OPTIMAL REGULATORY STRATEGIES

We calculated optimal regulatory strategies using stochastic dynamic programming (Lubow 1995, Johnson and Williams 1999). For the three western Flyways, we based this optimization on: (1) the 2007 regulatory alternatives, including the closed-season constraint; (2) current population models and associated weights for mid-continent mallards; and (3) the dual objectives of maximizing long-term cumulative harvest and achieving a population goal of 8.8 million mid-continent mallards. The resulting regulatory strategy (Table 9) is similar to that used last year. Note that prescriptions for closed seasons in this strategy represent resource conditions that are insufficient to support one of the current regulatory alternatives, given current harvest-management objectives and constraints. However, closed seasons under all of these conditions are not necessarily required for long-term resource protection, and simply reflect the NAWMP population goal and the nature of the current regulatory alternatives. Assuming that regulatory choices adhered to this strategy (and that current model weights accurately reflect population dynamics), breeding-population size would be expected to average 7.45 million (SD = 1.81 million). Based on an estimated population size of 9.05 million mid-continent mallards and 5.04 million ponds in Prairie Canada, the optimal choice for the Pacific, Central, and Mississippi Flyways in 2007 is the liberal regulatory alternative.

We calculated an optimal regulatory strategy for the Atlantic Flyway based on: (1) the 2007 regulatory alternatives; (2) current population models and associated weights for eastern mallards; and (3) an objective to maximize long-term cumulative harvest. The resulting strategy suggests liberal regulations for all population sizes of record, and is characterized by a lack of intermediate regulations (Table 10). We simulated the use of this regulatory strategy to determine expected performance characteristics. Assuming that harvest management adhered to this strategy (and that current model weights accurately reflect population dynamics), breeding-population size would be expected to average 887 thousand (SD = 16 thousand). Based on an estimated breeding population size of 907 thousand mallards, the optimal choice for the Atlantic Flyway in 2007 is the liberal regulatory alternative.

Table 9. Optimal regulatory strategy[a] for the three western Flyways for the 2007 hunting season. This strategy is based on current regulatory alternatives (including the closed-season constraint), on current mid-continent mallard models and weights, and on the dual objectives of maximizing long-term cumulative harvest and achieving a population goal of 8.8 million mallards. The shaded cell indicates the regulatory prescription for 2007.

| Bpop[b] | Ponds[c] | | | | | | | | | |
|---------|-----|-----|-----|-----|-----|-----|-----|-----|-----|-----|
| | 1.5 | 2.0 | 2.5 | 3.0 | 3.5 | 4.0 | 4.5 | 5.0 | 5.5 | 6.0 |
| ≤5.25 | C | C | C | C | C | C | C | C | C | C |
| 5.50-6.25 | R | R | R | R | R | R | R | R | R | R |
| 6.50 | R | R | R | R | R | R | R | R | M | M |
| 6.75 | R | R | R | R | R | R | M | M | M | L |
| 7.00 | R | R | R | R | R | M | M | L | L | L |
| 7.25 | R | R | R | M | L | L | L | L | L | L |
| 7.50 | R | M | M | L | L | L | L | L | L | L |
| 7.75 | M | M | M | L | L | L | L | L | L | L |
| 8.00 | M | L | L | L | L | L | L | L | L | L |
| ≥8.25 | L | L | L | L | L | L | L | L | L | L |

[a] C = closed season, R = restrictive, M = moderate, L = liberal.
[b] Mallard breeding population size (in millions) in the traditional survey area (survey strata 1-18, 20-50, 75-77) and Michigan, Minnesota, and Wisconsin.
[c] Ponds (in millions) in Prairie Canada in May.

Table 10. Optimal regulatory strategy[a] for the Atlantic Flyway for the 2007 hunting season. This strategy is based on current regulatory alternatives, on current eastern mallard models and weights, and on an objective to maximize long-term cumulative harvest. The shaded cell indicates the regulatory prescription for 2007.

| Mallards[b] | Regulation |
|-------------|------------|
| <240 | C |
| 240 | R |
| >240 | L |

[a] C = closed season, R = restrictive, M = moderate, and L = liberal.
[b] Estimated number of mallards in eastern Canada (survey strata 51-54, 56) and the northeastern U.S. (state plot surveys), in thousands.

# Application of AHM Concepts to Other Stocks

The USFWS is striving to apply the principles and tools of AHM to improve decision-making for several other stocks of waterfowl. We report on four such efforts in which significant progress has been made since last year.

## American Black Ducks

Beginning in 2003 the USFWS Division of Migratory Bird Management (DMBM) began investigating optimal harvest strategies for black ducks based on models of population dynamics provided by Conroy et al (2002). As a result of that investigation DMBM concluded that recent harvest rates of black ducks have sometimes been at or above levels consistent with an objective to maximize sustainable harvest. That conclusion ultimately led to a DMBM recommendation in January 2006 to reduce the harvest rate of adult black ducks by 25%. However, the recommendation was subsequently withdrawn because of: (1) published information suggesting that the mid-winter inventory (MWI) may be "capturing" a smaller proportion of the black duck population than in the past (Link et al. 2006); (2) concern about the U.S. acting unilaterally without the benefit of consultation with the CWS; and (3) the short amount of time available to communicate to the public the rationale and nature of restrictions on hunting opportunity.

In November 2006 the international Black Duck Adaptive Harvest Management Working Group (BDAHMWG) met to discuss the most recent analysis by Drs. Mike Conroy and Jon Runge of the Georgia Cooperative Fish and Wildlife Research Unit. Their update of the original analysis by Conroy et al. (2002) suggests that black duck productivity has continued to decline for reasons that cannot be explained by changes in abundance of black ducks (through density dependence) or sympatric mallards (through inter-species competition). However, there were other differences in inferences based on the original and updated analyses that could not be reconciled. The focus of research has now turned to population models based on integrated fixed-wing and helicopter surveys conducted during the breeding season. For the present, however, the question of whether current harvest rates of black ducks are consistent with black duck harvest potential and management objectives remains unanswered.

Due to potential changes in the wintering distribution of black ducks, the BDAHMWG did not endorse a state-dependent harvest strategy (i.e., one in which optimal harvest rates depend on annual black duck abundance) based on the MWI. However, it was suggested that a constant harvest-rate strategy may perform nearly as well and might provide a basis for a joint Canada-U.S. harvest strategy until an assessment based on breeding-season surveys can be completed. The BDAHMWG agreed to investigate the performance of constant harvest-rate strategies based on the original work of Conroy et al. (2002), recognizing that the original analysis was conducted prior to what may be significant changes in the wintering distribution of black ducks. Thus, it was agreed that the assessment by Conroy et al. (2002) might still provide a reasonable basis for investigating harvest impacts and for evaluating the expected performance of constant harvest-rate strategies.

We relied on the population models and corresponding weights provided by Conroy et al. (2002) to conduct an evaluation of constant harvest-rate strategies. These models incorporate alternative hypotheses for reproduction (competition with mallards vs. no competition), survival (additive vs. compensatory hunting mortality), and estimation bias (positive bias in reproductive rates vs. survival rates). Both reproduction models incorporate a negative effect of year, presumably due to a long-term loss and/or degradation of habitat. For the purposes of this assessment we projected the log-linear decline in production rate through 2007. We believe this was justified because of evidence that the decline in productivity has continued to the present at about the same rate as that estimated from the 1961-1994 period. However, for the purposes of this assessment we had to assume that the decline in productivity halts in 2007. To project the decline indefinitely into the future would imply that no level of harvest is sustainable. Managers are currently considering plausible explanations for the productivity decline, and will need to be vigilant in assessing future trends in productivity.

Because of the possible effect of mallard abundance on black duck productivity, it was necessary to include a dynamic model of mallard abundance ($M$). The model used by Conroy et al. (2002) was:

$$M_{t+1} = M_t \lambda_t$$

where $\lambda_t$ is the finite rate of population growth. Estimates of $\lambda_t$ from 1971-1994 were used to obtain an empirical distribution to specify random outcomes for $\lambda_t$. During 1971-1994 $\lambda_t$ was highly variable, but with an average close to 1 (suggestive of a stable population).

We were not completely satisfied with this model because it can produce biologically unrealistic changes in population size (because population size and $\lambda_t$ are uncorrelated) and because population size had to be constrained to an arbitrary maximum. Therefore, we described changes in mallard abundance as a $1^{st}$-order autoregressive process using data from 1971-2000. The model is:

$$M_{t+1}(0.00001) = 1.801 + 0.494(M_t(0.00001)) + e$$

where

$$e \sim Normal(0, 0.300).$$

This model provided a satisfactory fit to the time series of observed population sizes and describes a stationary time series with $\overline{M}_t = 355,826$.

We evaluated constant harvest-rate strategies using SDP (Lubow 1995) and by constraining the size of the harvest to be equal in Canada and the U.S. We specified fixed harvest rates of 0.00 to 0.16 in increments of 0.01. We simulated black duck and mallard population dynamics for 20,000 iterations under each of the fixed harvest rates, using starting values of 300k black ducks and 356k mallards. We then calculated the mean and standard deviation of black duck population size and harvest. For comparative purposes, we also derived an optimal state-dependent harvest strategy using SDP and an objective to maximize long-term cumulative harvest.

Based on simulated population dynamics, the black duck population averaged 546k (SD = 154k) in the absence of harvest (Fig. 7). An optimal state-dependent strategy to maximize sustainable harvest (i.e., a strategy in which the harvest rate varies with black duck abundance) resulted in an average population size of 255k (SD = 50k) and an average harvest of 51K (SD = 41k). For a constant harvest rate, the maximum sustainable harvest was achieved at a harvest rate of 0.09 on adult males, resulting in an average of 240k (SD = 94k) black ducks in the MWI and a harvest of 47k (SD = 15k). Thus, the expected harvest under a constant harvest-rate strategy was only 7% less than that which could be achieved under an optimal state-dependent harvest strategy. However, population size was nearly twice as variable under the constant harvest rate of 0.09 as under the optimal state-dependent strategy.

For a target harvest rate of 0.09, the corresponding harvest rates in Canada and the U.S. to achieve parity in harvest are 0.045 and 0.048, respectively. By comparison, adult black duck harvest rates estimated from reward banding during the 2002-2006 hunting seasons averaged 0.0358 (SE = 0.00073) for Canada, 0.0584 (SE = 0.0017) for the U.S., and 0.0916 (SE = 0.0016) overall. The average population size in the MWI during 2003-2007 of 220k corresponds well with that predicted from the weighted models under an average harvest rate of 0.09 (240k).

A harvest rate of 0.09 should be considered a maximum because it assumes that black duck productivity will not decline further. Moreover, a smaller harvest rate appears to be necessary to induce population growth. For example, attainment of the original North American Waterfowl Management Plan population objective of 385k black ducks in the MWI would require a constant harvest rate of approximately 0.05 under current environmental conditions.

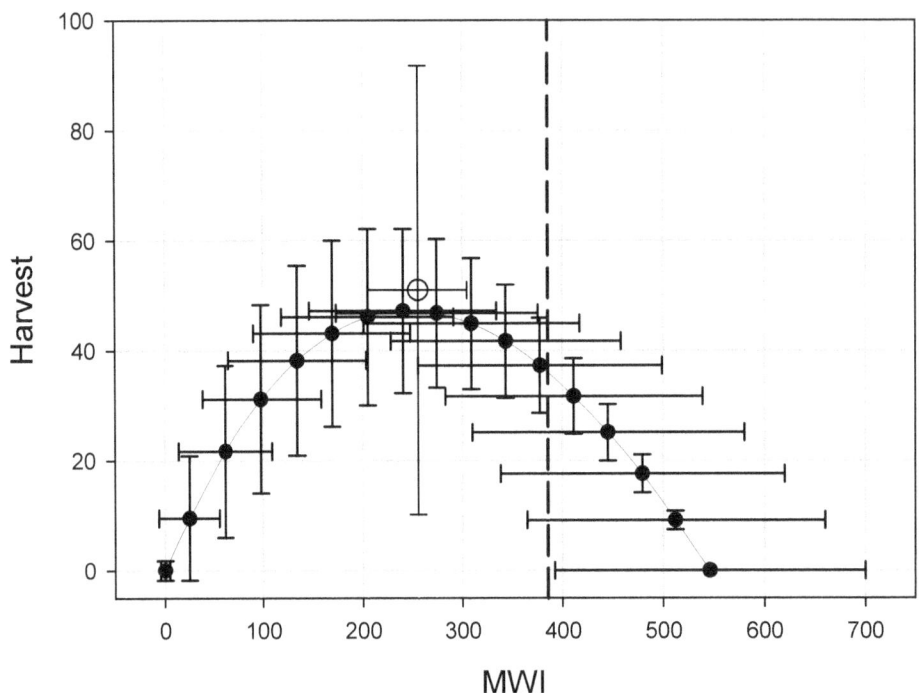

Fig. 7. Black duck population sizes in winter (MWI) and harvests (both in thousands, with SD's) expected under constant adult-male harvest rates of 0.00 (on the extreme right) to 0.16 (on the extreme left) in increments of 0.01. The datum depicted by the open circle is that expected under an optimal state-dependent strategy with an objective to maximize long-term cumulative harvest. The vertical dashed line indicates the original North American Waterfowl Management Plan population goal of 385 thousand.

## Atlantic Population of Canada Geese

For the purposes of this AHM application, Atlantic Population Canada Geese (APCG) are defined as those geese breeding on the Ungava Peninsula. By this delineation, we assume that geese in the Atlantic population outside this area are either few in number, similar in population dynamics to the Ungava birds, or both.

To account for heterogeneity among individuals, we developed a base model consisting of a truncated time-invariant age-based projection model to describe the dynamics of APCG:

$$\mathbf{n}(t+1)=\mathbf{A}\mathbf{n}(t),$$

where $\mathbf{n}(t)$ is a vector of the abundances of the ages in the population at time $t$, and $\mathbf{A}$ is the population projection matrix, whose $ij$th entry $a_{ij}$ gives the contribution of an individual in stage $j$ to stage $i$ over 1 time step. The projection interval (from $t$ to $t+1$) is one year, with the census being taken in mid-June (i.e., this model has a pre-breeding census). The life cycle diagram reflecting the transition sequence is:

20

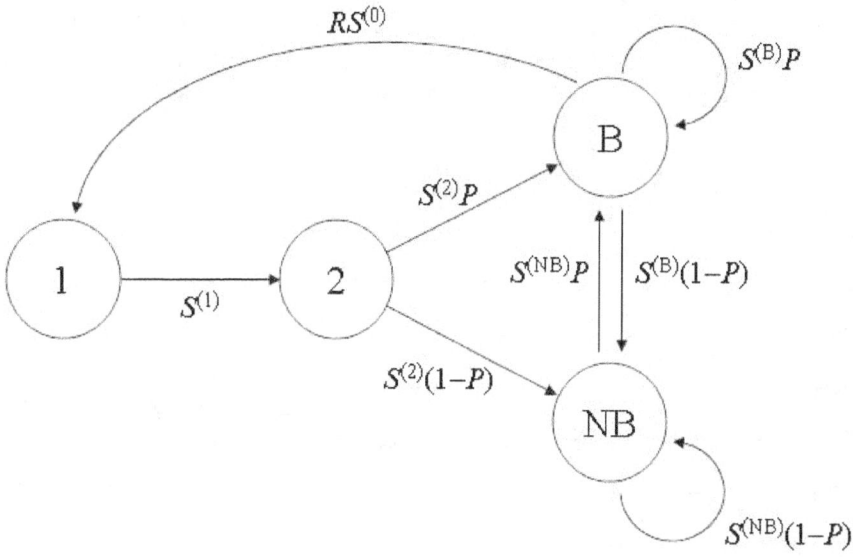

where node 1 refers to one-year-old birds ($N^{(1)}$), node 2 refers to two-year-old birds ($N^{(2)}$), node B refers to adult breeders ($N^{(B)}$), and node NB refers to adult non-breeders $N^{(NB)}$. One immediate extension of the base model is to remove the assumption of time-invariance, and express the parameters as time-dependent quantities:

$P_t$ = proportion of adult birds in population in year $t$ which breed;

$R_t$ = basic breeding productivity in year $t$ (per capita);

$S_t^{(0)}$ = annual survival rate of young from fledging in year $t$ to the census point the next year;

$S_t^{(1)}$ = annual survival rate of one-year-old birds in year $t$; etc.

For APCG, only $N^{(B)}$, $R$ and $z$ are observable annually, where $N^{(B)}$ is the number of breeding adults, $R$ is the per capita reproductive rate (ratio of fledged young to breeding adults), and $z$ is an extrinsic, environmental variable (a function of timing of snow melt on the breeding grounds) that is used to predict $R$..

Note that at the time of the management decision in the United States (July), estimates for only the breeding population size and the environmental variable(s) are available; the age-ratio isn't estimated until later in the summer. Thus, in year $t$, the observable state variables are $N_t^{(B)}$, $z_t$, and $R_{t-1}$.

There are several other state variables of interest, however, namely, $N^{(1)}$, $N^{(2)}$, and $N^{(NB)}$. Because annual harvest decisions need to be made based on the total population size ($N^{tot}$), which is the sum of contributions from various non-breeding age classes as well as the number of breeding individuals, abundance of non-breeding individuals ($N^{(NB)}$, $N^{(1)}$, and $N^{(2)}$) needs to be derived using population-reconstruction techniques. In most cases, population reconstruction involves estimating the most likely population projection matrix, given a time series of population vectors (where number of individuals in each age class at each time is known). However, in our case, only estimates of $N^B$, $R$ and $z$ are available (not the complete population vector); in effect, we must estimate some of the population abundance values given the other parameters in the model. Extensions of Bayesian and nonlinear estimation methods to population reconstruction provide a reasonable solution.

The time series of breeding population size, age-ratio, and harvest rate were used to reconstruct the population structure from 1997 to the present, using a density-independent model (Fig. 8). The estimated population structure in 2007 is: 382,100 breeding adults, 99,300 non-breeding adults, 235,900 second-year birds, and 342,200 first-year birds. Relative to the number of breeding adults, second-year birds are 29.0% above the number expected from a stable stage-distribution, and first-year birds are 35.9% above the expected number, reflecting the impact of the very successful 2005 and 2006 breeding seasons. The density-independent model projects significant increases in the number of breeding pairs (~25% over the next two years) as these two sizeable cohorts come of age.

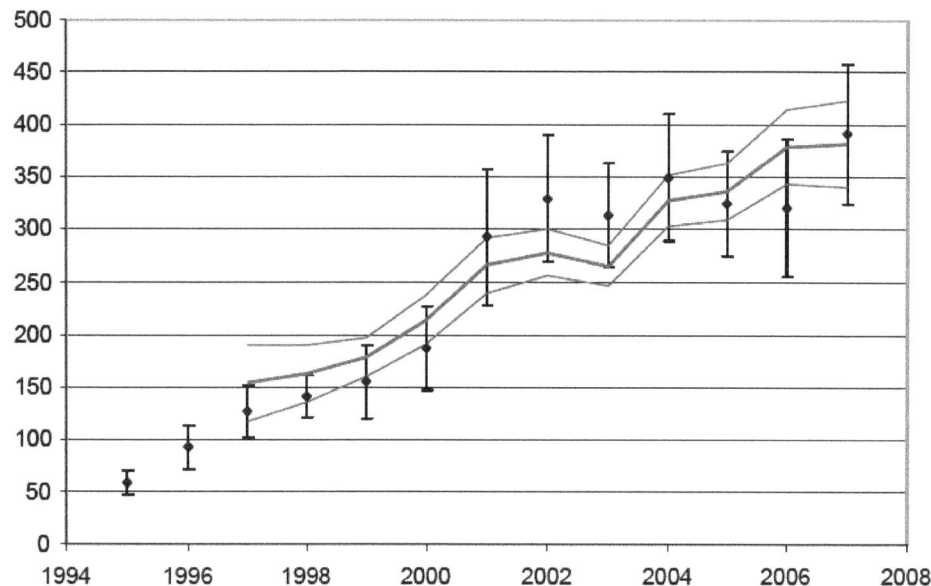

Fig. 8. APCG breeding population size (in thousands), 1993-2007, with fitted values from reconstruction (Model 1: density-independent). The diamonds show the observed estimates of breeding population size (not breeding pairs); errors bars are ±2 SE. The solid line shows the breeding population size estimated from the population reconstruction (also ±2 SE). The observed 1998 population size was smoothed because the survey conditions were poor.

Based on the data available last year, we had postulated several alternative models to explain the apparent stabilization in the population trajectory. The three alternative models included mechanisms for density-dependent survival, density-dependent propensity to breed, and reporting rate bias. With the 2007 breeding survey data included, the differences among the trajectories for these models diminished, but the reconstructed age-structure of the current population differs substantially among them, as do the optimal harvest strategies.

As an example, harvest strategies for two of the population models are shown in Fig. 9. With the density-independent model, the strategy seeks an equilibrium breeding population size of 748,500. The strategy suggests a closed season this year, in order to increase more quickly toward the desired population size. On the other hand, the optimal strategy for the density-dependent model seeks an equilibrium breeding population size of 308,000 and because the current population size is above that, the recommended hunting regulations are liberal (20% harvest rate). Note that in both strategies, the recommended harvest rate is not strongly affected by the measure of current environmental conditions on the breeding grounds.

Thus, harvest recommendations are strongly affected by uncertainty about the underlying population dynamics. We have not yet developed methods to weight the alternative models and produce a composite optimal policy; such development is a high priority. However, this population is in a very informative phase of its dynamics, such that each year of data greatly increases our ability to distinguish among alternative models.

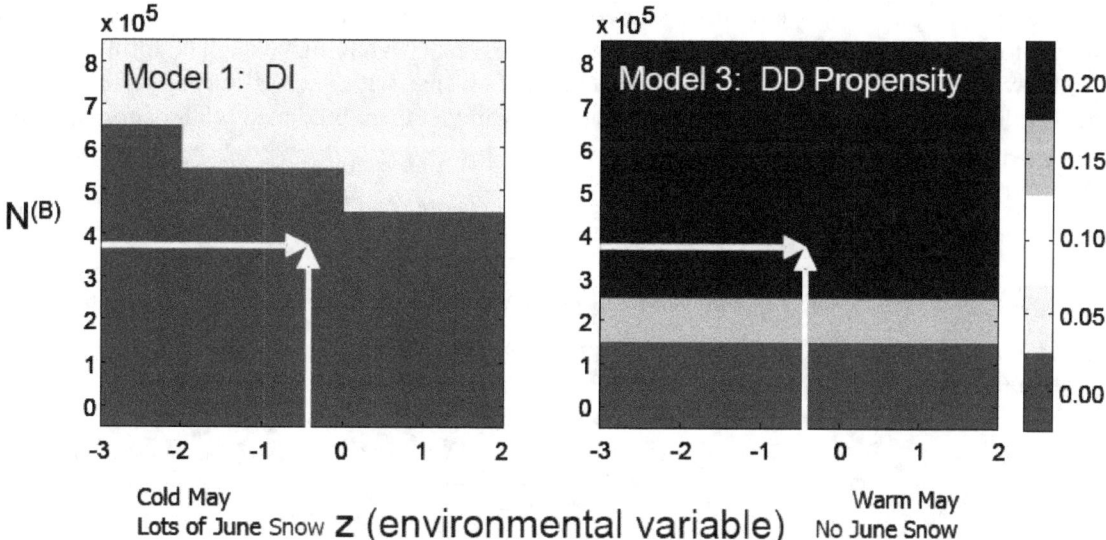

Fig. 9. Examples of optimal harvest strategies for 2007 for models 1 (density-independent) and 3 (density-dependent breeding propensity). These matrices show the breeding population size against the measure of breeding habitat conditions (principal component of the weather variables), with the other values of the population vector ($N^{NB}$, $N^2$, $N^1$) fixed at their 2007 reconstructed values. The shaded areas represent the recommended harvest rate of adult males.

## Northern Pintails

The Flyway Councils have long identified the northern pintail as a high-priority species for inclusion in the AHM process. In 1997, the USFWS adopted a pintail harvest strategy to help align harvest opportunity with population status, while providing a foundation upon which to develop a formal AHM framework. Since 1997, the harvest strategy has undergone a number of technical improvements and policy revisions. However, the strategy continues to be a set of regulatory prescriptions born out of consensus, rather than an optimal strategy derived from agreed-upon population models, management objectives, regulatory alternatives, and measures of uncertainty.

This year, the USFWS and Flyway Councils are taking a major step towards a truly adaptive approach by incorporating alternative models of population dynamics. Two models are being considered: one in which harvest is additive to natural mortality, and another in which harvest losses are compensated for by reductions in natural mortality. In the additive model, winter survival rate is a constant, whereas winter survival is density-dependent in the compensatory model. We here provide a summary of these recent modeling efforts. A detailed progress report is available on-line at http://www.fws.gov/migratorybirds/mgmt/ahm/special-topics.htm.

The predicted $cBPOPt$ in year $t + 1$ ($cBPOP_{t+1}$) for the additive harvest mortality model is calculated as

$$cBPOP_{t+1} = \left\{ cBPOP_t s_s (1 + \gamma_R \hat{R}_t) - \hat{H}_t /(1-c) \right\} s_w$$

where $cBPOP_t$ is the latitude-adjusted breeding population size in year $t$, $s_s$ and $s_w$ are the summer and winter survival rates, respectively, $\gamma_R$ is a bias-correction constant for the age-ratio, $c$ is the crippling loss rate, $\hat{R}_t$ is the predicted age-ratio, and $\hat{H}_t$ is the predicted continental harvest. Discussion of $\hat{R}_t$ and $\hat{H}_t$ submodels are found in the following sections. The model uses the following constants: $s_s = 0.07$, $s_w = 0.93$, $\gamma_R = 0.8$, and $c = 0.20$.

The compensatory harvest mortality model serves as a hypothesis that stands in contrast to the additive harvest

23

mortality model, positing a strong but realistic degree of compensation. The compensatory model assumes that the mechanism for compensation is density-dependent post-harvest (winter) survival. The form is a logistic relationship between winter survival and post-harvest population size, with the relationship anchored around the historic mean values for each variable. For the compensatory model then, predicted winter survival rate in year $t$ ($s_t$) is calculated as

$$s_t = s_0 + (s_1 - s_0)\left[1 + e^{-(a+b(P_t - \overline{P}))}\right]^{-1},$$

where $s_1$ (upper asymptote) is 1.0, $s_0$ (lower asymptote) is 0.7, $b$ (slope term) is -1.0, $P_t$ is the post-harvest population size in year $t$ (expressed in millions), $\overline{P}$ is the mean post-harvest population size (4.295 million from 1974 through 2005), and

$$a = \text{logit}\left(\frac{\overline{s} - s_0}{s_1 - s_0}\right)$$

or

$$a = \log\left(\frac{\overline{s} - s_0}{s_1 - s_0}\right) - \log\left\{1 - \left(\frac{\overline{s} - s_0}{s_1 - s_0}\right)\right\},$$

where $\overline{s}$ is 0.93 (mean winter survival rate).

At moderate population size and latitude, the compensatory model allows for greater harvest (Fig. 10) than does the additive model (note especially that the size of the restrictive region [season-within-a-season] is smaller and is invoked when the latitude is higher). Also, 2- and 3-bird bag limits are called for under more circumstances. But, at high population sizes, the higher bag limits are called for less often, because the compensatory model predicts that growth of the population will be slower (density-dependence).

The fit to historic data was used to compare the additive and compensatory harvest models. From the $cBPOP_t$, $mLAT_t$, and observed harvest ($H_t$) for the period 1974–through year $t$, the subsequent year's breeding population size (on the latitude-adjusted scale) was predicted with both the additive and compensatory model, and compared to the observed breeding population size (on the latitude-adjusted scale). The mean-squared error of the predictions from the additive model ($MSE_{add}$) was calculated as:

$$MSE_{add} = \frac{1}{(t-1975)+1} \sum_{t=1975}^{t} (cBPOP_t - cBPOP_t^{add})^2$$

and the mean-squared error of the predictions from the compensatory model were calculated in a similar manner.

The model weights for the additive and compensatory model were calculated from their relative mean-squared errors. The model weight for the additive model ($W_{add}$) was calculated as:

$$W_{add} = \frac{\dfrac{1}{MSE_{add}}}{\dfrac{1}{MSE_{add}} + \dfrac{1}{MSE_{comp}}}.$$

The model weight for the compensatory model was found in a corresponding manner, or by subtracting the additive model weight from 1.0. As of 2006, the compensatory model did not fit the historic data as well as the additive model; the model weights were 0.597 for the additive model and 0.403 for the compensatory model. The 2006 average model calls for a strategy that is intermediate between the additive and compensatory models (Fig. 10).

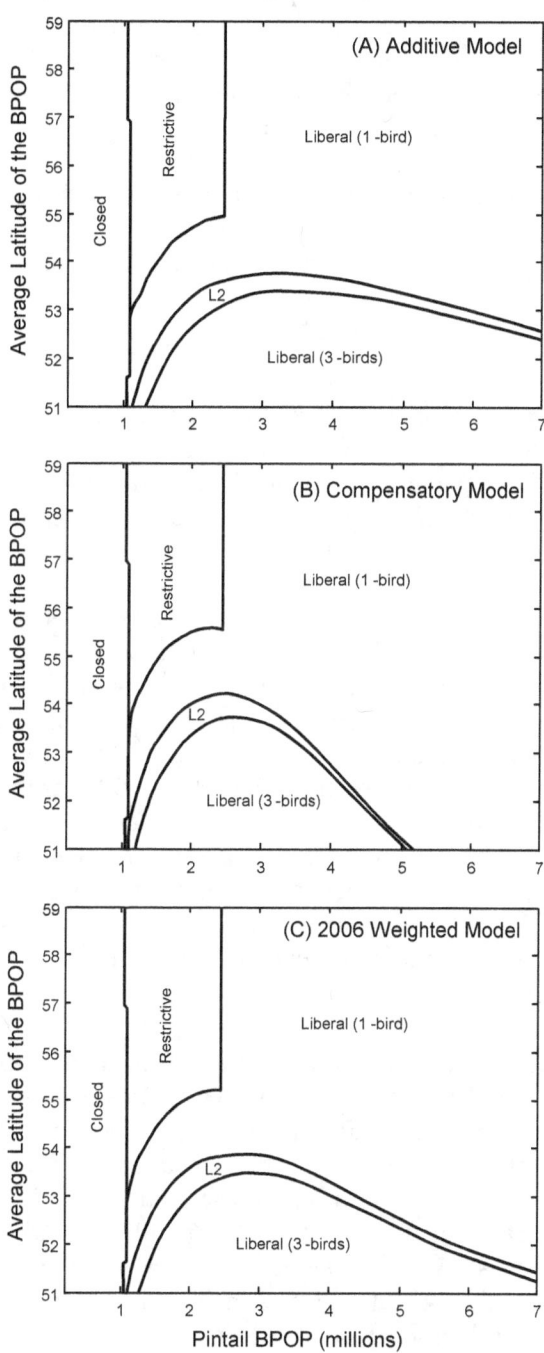

Fig. 10. State-dependent harvest strategy for northern pintails with (A) additive, (B) compensatory, and (C) 2006 weighted models. In each case the strategy assumes that the general duck hunting season is that prescribed under the liberal regulatory alternative.

# Scaup

The continental scaup (greater and lesser combined) population has experienced a long-term decline (Austin *et al.* 2000, Afton and Anderson 2001, Austin *et al.* 2006). As a result, waterfowl managers are challenged with the issue of how to manage the harvest of this declining population in the absence of an objective harvest strategy. In response to this dilemma, the USFWS Migratory Bird Regulations Committee requested that a scaup harvest strategy be developed for the 2007 regulations cycle. Here, we report on the development of a proposed decision-making framework to guide scaup harvest management. A detailed report is available on-line at http://www.fws.gov/migratorybirds/mgmt/ahm/special-topics.htm.

The lack of scaup demographic information over a sufficient timeframe and at a continental scale precludes the use of a traditional balance equation to represent scaup population and harvest dynamics. As a result, we used a discrete-time, stochastic, logistic-growth population model to represent changes in scaup abundance:

$$N_t = (N_{t-1} + rN_{t-1}(1 - N_{t-1} / K) - qH_{t-1})e^{\varepsilon_t}.$$

With this formulation, annual changes in population size ($N$) are predicted by the intrinsic rate of increase ($r$), the carrying capacity ($K$), a scaled harvest ($H$), and a process error ($\varepsilon$). We use a Bayesian approach (Meyer and Millar 1999) to estimate the population parameters, and to characterize the uncertainty associated with the monitoring programs (observation error) and the ability of our model to predict actual changes in the system (process error).

Our initial assessment relied on the critical assumption that data used to estimate population parameters were measured on the same absolute scale. Research conducted to model waterfowl populations from different sources of information has provided evidence of bias in waterfowl survey programs (Martin *et al.* 1979, Runge *et al.* 2002). While the source(s) of this bias are not yet known, it is possible to estimate correction factors to reconcile predictions based on disparate sources of information. To address this issue, we chose to include an additional parameter ($q$) in our assessment to function as a scaling factor that enables us to combine breeding population and harvest estimates in an expression of population change. It is important to note that this parameter represents the combined limitations and uncertainty of all the monitoring data and functional relationships used in our assessment framework. Although, our initial attempts to estimate a scaling parameter from population and harvest data yielded reasonable estimates, the variance estimates were large. We found that the inclusion of a limited amount of scaup banding and recovery data provided enough information to structure the harvest process and reduce the uncertainty in the scaling parameter estimate.

As in past analyses, the state space formulation and Bayesian analysis framework provided reasonable fits to the observed breeding population and total harvest estimates with realistic measures of variation. The posterior mean harvest rate estimates ranged from 0.03 to 0.08. In general, harvest rates fluctuated over the first decade and then tracked the declining population trend until the early 1990's, when harvest rate estimates increased significantly before dropping in 1999 (Fig. 11). The posterior mean estimate of the intrinsic rate of increase ($r$) is 0.110 while the posterior mean estimate of the carrying capacity ($K$) is 8.236 million birds (Table 1). The posterior mean estimate of the scaling parameter ($q$) is 0.541, ranging between 0.461 and 0.630 with 95% probability. Based on the estimated population parameters, the estimated average maximum sustainable yield (MSY) on the adjusted scale is 0.211 million scaup (0.389 million scaup on the observed scale).

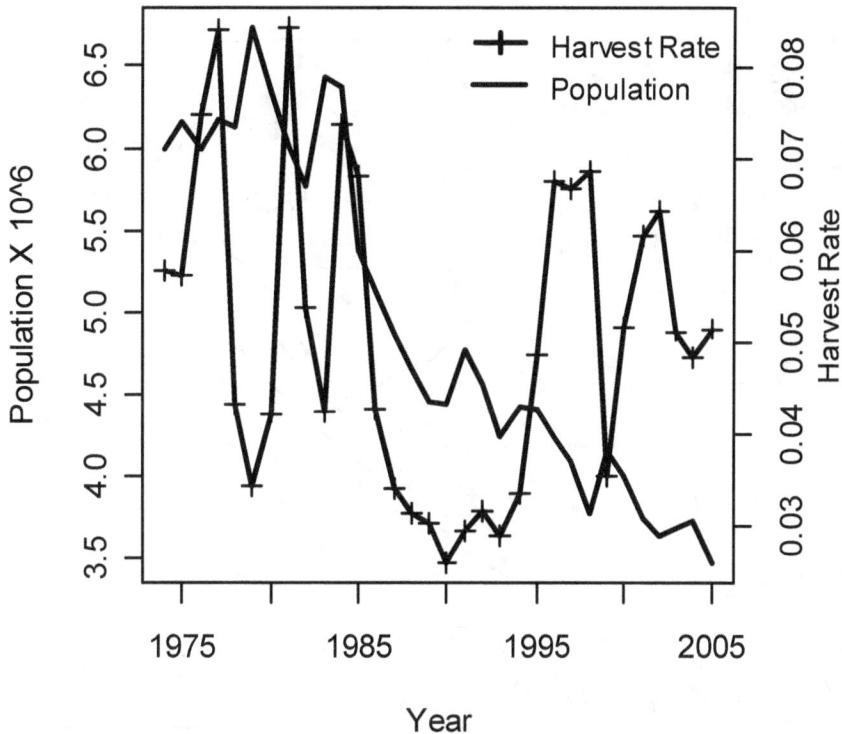

Fig. 11. The posterior mean scaup population and harvest rate estimates derived from a Bayesian analysis of the modified logistic model.

We used SDP software (Lubow 1995) to derive a state-dependent harvest strategy under an objective to maximize long-term cumulative harvest (MSY) and an objective to attain a shoulder point (calculated as percentage of MSY) on the yield curve. We evaluated harvest levels from 0 to 5 million (in increments of 50,000) for population sizes of 1 to 10 million (in increments of 50,000) and harvest objectives ranging from 90 to 100% MSY (in 2 % increments). For each optimization we assumed perfect control over the harvest decision variable. We then simulated each strategy for 5000 iterations to characterize the management performance expected if the harvest strategy was followed and system dynamics did not change.

Under an objective to maximize long-term cumulative harvest (MSY) the resulting strategy is extremely knife-edged (Fig. 12). This strategy prescribes zero harvests for population sizes less than 3.2 million and seeks to hold the population size at maximum productivity (one half the carrying capacity). In contrast to the MSY strategy, the harvest strategies necessary to achieve a shoulder point are considerably less knife-edged and would allow for harvest at lower population sizes. However, current scaup harvest levels (317,000) exceed the prescribed harvests resulting from optimizations with each of the objective functions we evaluated. The simulated management performance of each harvest strategy demonstrates the tradeoffs that arise when a shoulder point objective is used to derive an optimal harvest strategy. As the desired shoulder point moves away from MSY, average harvest levels decrease while the average population increases.

The USFWS intends to work with the Flyways over the next year to determine an acceptable harvest-management objective and a set of regulatory alternatives that would be used in conjunction with our modeling framework to derive an optimal harvest strategy for scaup.

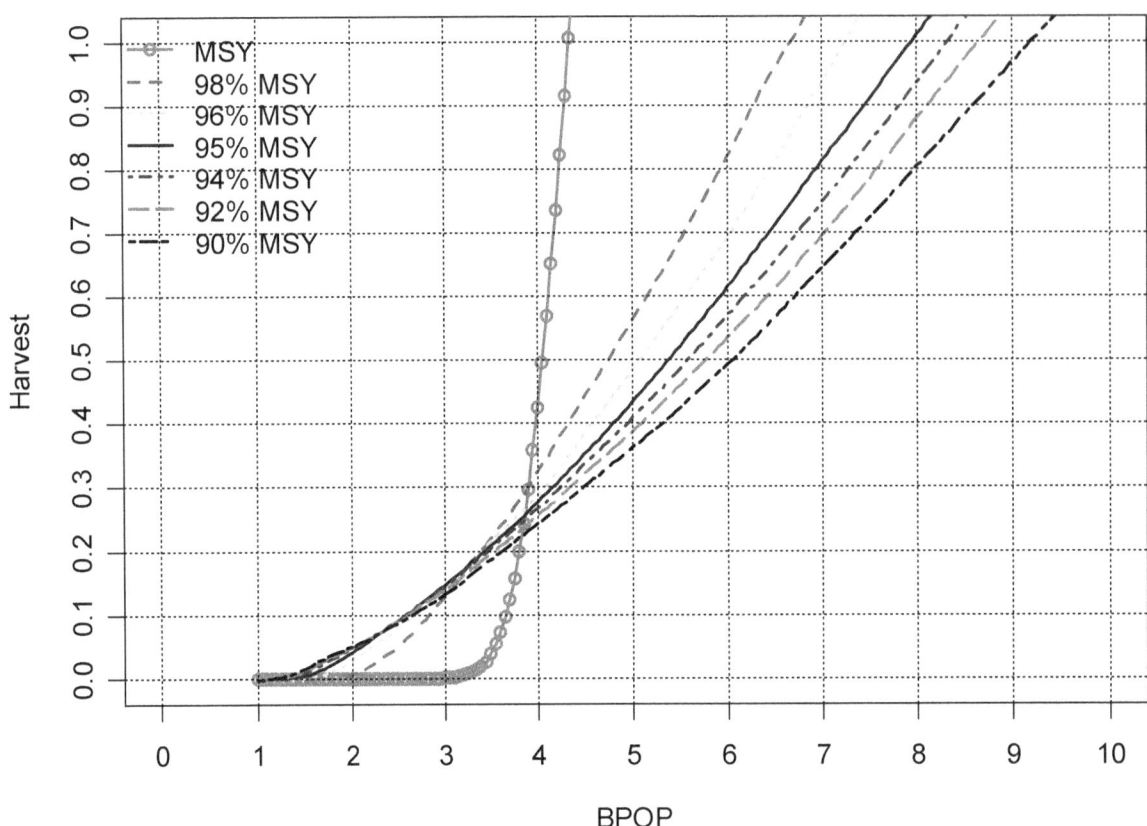

Fig. 12. Optimal harvests of scaup as a function of the observed breeding population size derived under objective functions ranging from 90 to 100 percent of the maximum long-term yield (MSY).

# LITERATURE CITED

Afton, A. D., and M. G. Anderson. 2001. Declining scaup populations: a retrospective analysis of long-term population and harvest survey data. Journal of Wildlife Management 60:83-93.

Anderson, D. R., and K. P. Burnham. 1976. Population ecology of the mallard. VI. The effect of exploitation on survival. U.S. Fish and Wildlife Service Resource Publication No. 128. 66pp.

Austin, J. E., A. D. Afton, M. G. Anderson, R. G. Clark, C. M. Custer, J. S. Lawrence, J. B. Pollard and J. K. Ringelman. 2000. Declining scaup populations: issues, hypotheses, and research needs. Wildlife Society Bulletin 28:254-263.

Austin, J. E., M. J. Anteau, J. S. Barclay, G. S. Boomer, F. C. Rohwer, and S. M. Slattery. 2006. Declining scaup populations: reassessment of the issues, hypotheses, and research directions. Consensus Report from the Second Scaup Workshop. 7pp.

Blohm, R. J. 1989. Introduction to harvest - understanding surveys and season setting. Proceedings of the International Waterfowl Symposium 6:118-133.

Blohm, R. J., R. E. Reynolds, J. P. Bladen, J. D. Nichols, J. E. Hines, K. P. Pollock, and R. T. Eberhardt. 1987. Mallard mortality rates on key breeding and wintering areas. Transactions of the North American Wildlife and Natural Resources Conference 52:246-263.

Burnham, K. P., G. C. White, and D. R. Anderson. 1984. Estimating the effect of hunting on annual survival rates of adult mallards. Journal of Wildlife Management 48:350-361.

Conroy, M. J., M. W. Miller, and J. E. Hines. 2002. Identification and synthetic modeling of factors affecting American black duck populations. Wildlife Monographs 150. 64pp.

Heusman, H W, and J. R. Sauer. 2000. The northeastern states' waterfowl breeding population survey. Wildlife Society Bulletin 28:355-364.

Johnson, F. A. 2003. Population dynamics of ducks other than mallards in mid-continent North America. Draft. Fish and Wildlife Service, U.S. Dept. Interior, Washington, D.C. 15pp.

Johnson, F. A., J. A. Dubovsky, M. C. Runge, and D. R. Eggeman. 2002a. A revised protocol for the adaptive harvest management of eastern mallards. Fish and Wildlife Service, U.S. Dept. Interior, Washington, D.C. 13pp. [online] URL: http://migratorybirds.fws.gov/reports/ahm02/emal-ahm-2002.pdf.

Johnson, F. A., W. L. Kendall, and J. A. Dubovsky. 2002b. Conditions and limitations on learning in the adaptive management of mallard harvests. Wildlife Society Bulletin 30:176-185.

Johnson, F. A., C. T. Moore, W. L. Kendall, J. A. Dubovsky, D. F. Caithamer, J. R. Kelley, Jr., and B. K. Williams. 1997. Uncertainty and the management of mallard harvests. Journal of Wildlife Management 61:202-216.

Johnson, F. A., and B. K. Williams. 1999. Protocol and practice in the adaptive management of waterfowl harvests. Conservation Ecology 3(1): 8. [online] URL: http://www.consecol.org/vol3/iss1/art8.

Johnson, F. A., B. K. Williams, J. D. Nichols, J. E. Hines, W. L. Kendall, G. W. Smith, and D. F. Caithamer. 1993. Developing an adaptive management strategy for harvesting waterfowl in North America. Transactions of the North American Wildlife and Natural Resources Conference 58:565-583.

Johnson, F. A., B. K. Williams, and P. R. Schmidt. 1996. Adaptive decision-making in waterfowl harvest and habitat management. Proceedings of the International Waterfowl Symposium 7:26-33.

Link, W. A., J. R. Sauer, and D. K. Niven. 2006. A hierarchical model for regional analysis of population change using Christmas bird count data, with application to the American black duck. The Condor 108:13-24.

Lubow, B. C. 1995. SDP: Generalized software for solving stochastic dynamic optimization problems. Wildlife Society Bulletin 23:738-742.

Martin, F. W., R. S. Pospahala, and J. D. Nichols. 1979. Assessment and population management of North American migratory birds. Pages 187-239 in J. Cairns, G. P. Patil, and W. E. Waters, eds., Environmental biomonitoring, assessment, prediction and management — certain case studies and related quantitative issues. Statistical Ecology, Vol. S11. International Cooperative Publishing House, Fairland, MD.

Meyer, R., and R. B. Millar. 1999. BUGS in Bayesian stock assessments. Canadian Journal of Fisheries and Aquatic Sciences 56:1078-1086.

Munro, R. E., and C. F. Kimball. 1982. Population ecology of the mallard. VII. Distribution and derivation of the harvest. U.S. Fish and Wildlife Service Resource Publication 147. 127pp.

Nichols, J. D., F. A. Johnson, and B. K. Williams. 1995. Managing North American waterfowl in the face of uncertainty. Annual Review of Ecology and Systematics 26:177-199.

Runge, M. C., F. A. Johnson, J. A. Dubovsky, W. L. Kendall, J. Lawrence, and J. Gammonley. 2002. A revised protocol for the adaptive harvest management of mid-continent mallards. Fish and Wildlife Service, U.S. Dept. Interior, Washington, D.C. 28pp. [online] URL: http://migratorybirds.fws.gov/reports/ahm02/MCMrevise2002.pdf.

U.S. Fish and Wildlife Service. 2000. Adaptive harvest management: 2000 duck hunting season. U.S. Dept. Interior, Washington. D.C. 43pp. [online] URL: http://migratorybirds.fws.gov/reports/ahm00/ahm2000.pdf.

U.S. Fish and Wildlife Service. 2001. Framework-date extensions for duck hunting in the United States: projected impacts & coping with uncertainty, U.S. Dept. Interior, Washington, D.C. 8pp. [online] URL: http://migratorybirds.fws.gov/reports/ahm01/fwassess.pdf.

U.S. Fish and Wildlife Service. 2002. Adaptive harvest management: 2002 duck hunting season. U.S. Dept. Interior, Washington. D.C. 34pp. [online] URL: http://migratorybirds.fws.gov/reports/ahm02/2002-AHM-report.pdf.

Walters, C. J. 1986. Adaptive management of renewable resources. MacMillan Publ. Co., New York, N.Y. 374pp.

Williams, B. K., and F. A. Johnson. 1995. Adaptive management and the regulation of waterfowl harvests. Wildlife Society Bulletin 23:430-436.

Williams, B. K., F. A. Johnson, and K. Wilkins. 1996. Uncertainty and the adaptive management of waterfowl harvests. Journal of Wildlife Management 60:223-232.

# APPENDIX A:  AHM Working Group

(Note: This list includes only permanent members of the AHM Working Group.  Not listed here are numerous persons from federal and state agencies that assist the Working Group on an ad-hoc basis.)

## Coordinator:

*Fred Johnson*
U.S. Fish & Wildlife Service
Bldg. 810, University of Florida
P.O. Box 110485
Gainesville, FL 32611
phone: 352-392-5075
fax: 352-846-0841
e-mail: fred_a_johnson@fws.gov

## USFWS Representatives:

*Bob Blohm* (Region 9)
U.S. Fish and Wildlife Service
4401 N Fairfax Drive
MS MSP-4107
Arlington, VA 22203
phone: 703-358-1966
fax: 703-358-2272
e-mail: robert_blohm@fws.gov

*Brad Bortner* (Region 1)
U.S. Fish and Wildlife Service
911 NE 11th Ave.
Portland, OR 97232-4181
phone: 503-231-6164
fax: 503-231-2364
e-mail: brad_bortner@fws.gov

*Dave Case* (contractor)
D.J. Case & Associates
607 Lincolnway West
Mishawaka, IN  46544
phone: 574-258-0100
fax: 574-258-0189
e-mail: dave@djcase.com

*Jim Dubovsky* (Region 6)
U.S. Fish and Wildlife Service
P.O. Box 25486-DFC
Denver, CO 80225-0486
phone: 303-236-4403
fax: 303-236-8680
e-mail:james_dubovsky@fws.gov

*Jeff Haskins* (Region 2)
U.S. Fish and Wildlife Service
P.O. Box 1306
Albuquerque, NM 87103
phone: 505-248-6827 (ext 30)
fax: 505-248-7885
e-mail: jeff_haskins@fws.gov

*Jim Kelley*  (Region 9)
U.S. Fish and Wildlife Service
1 Federal Drive
Fort Snelling, MN 55111-0458
phone: 612-713-5409
fax: 612-713-5393
e-mail: james_r_kelley@fws.gov

*Sean Kelly* (Region 3)
U.S. Fish and Wildlife Service
1 Federal Drive
Ft. Snelling, MN 55111-4056
phone: 612-713-5470
fax: 612-713-5393
e-mail: sean_kelly@fws.gov

*Paul Padding* (Region 9)
U.S. Fish and Wildlife Service
11510 American Holly Drive
Laurel, MD  20708
phone: 301-497-5851
fax: 301-497-5885
e-mail: paul_padding@fws.gov

*Diane Pence* (Region 5)
U.S. Fish and Wildlife Service
300 Westgate Center Drive
Hadley, MA 01035-9589
phone: 413-253-8577
fax: 413-253-8424
e-mail: diane_pence@fws.gov

*Russ Oates* (Region 7)
U.S. Fish and Wildlife Service
1011 East Tudor Road
Anchorage, AK 99503-6119
phone: 907-786-3446
fax: 907-786-3641
e-mail: russ_oates@fws.gov

*Dave Sharp* (Region 9)
U.S. Fish and Wildlife Service
P.O. Box 25486, DFC
Denver, CO 80225-0486
phone: 303-275-2386
fax: 303-275-2384
e-mail: dave_sharp@fws.gov

*Bob Trost* (Region 9)
U.S. Fish and Wildlife Service
911 NE 11th Ave.
Portland, OR 97232-4181
phone: 503-231-6162
fax: 503-231-6228
e-mail: robert_trost@fws.gov

*David Viker* (Region 4)
U.S. Fish and Wildlife Service
1875 Century Blvd., Suite 345
Atlanta, GA 30345
phone: 404-679-7188
fax: 404-679-7285
e-mail: david_viker@fws.gov

## Canadian Wildlife Service Representatives:

*Dale Caswell*
Canadian Wildlife Service
123 Main St. Suite 150
Winnepeg, Manitoba, Canada R3C 4W2
phone: 204-983-5260
fax: 204-983-5248
e-mail: dale.caswell@ec.gc.ca

*Eric Reed*
Canadian Wildlife Service
351 St. Joseph Boulevard
Hull, QC K1A OH3, Canada
phone: 819-953-0294
fax: 819-953-6283
e-mail: eric.reed@ec.gc.ca

## Flyway Council Representatives:

*Scott Baker* (Mississippi Flyway)
Mississippi Dept. of Wildlife, Fisheries, and Parks
P.O. Box 378
Redwood, MS 39156
 phone: 601-661-0294
fax: 601-364-2209
e-mail: mahannah1@aol.com

*Diane Eggeman* (Atlantic Flyway)
Florida Fish and Wildlife Conservation Commission
8932 Apalachee Pkwy.
Tallahassee, FL 32311
phone: 850-488-5878
fax: 850-488-5884
e-mail: diane.eggeman@fwc.state.fl.us

*Mike Johnson* (Central Flyway)
North Dakota Game and Fish Department
100 North Bismarck Expressway
Bismarck, ND 58501-5095
phone: 701-328-6319
fax: 701-328-6352
e-mail: mjohnson@state.nd.us

*Don Kraege* (Pacific Flyway)
Washington Dept. of Fish and Wildlife
600 Capital Way North
Olympia. WA 98501-1091
phone: 360-902-2509
fax: 360-902-2162
e-mail: kraegdkk@dfw.wa.gov

**Bryan Swift**  (Atlantic Flyway)
Dept. Environmental Conservation
625 Broadway
Albany, NY 12233-4754
phone: 518-402-8866
fax: 518-402-9027 or 402-8925
e-mail: blswift@gw.dec.state.ny.us

**Mark Vrtiska** (Central Flyway)
Nebraska Game and Parks Commission
P.O. Box 30370
2200 North 33rd Street
Lincoln, NE 68503-1417
phone: 402-471-5437
fax: 402-471-5528
email: mvrtiska@ngpc.state.ne.us

**Dan Yparraguirre** (Pacific Flyway)
California Dept. of Fish and Game
1812 Ninth Street
Sacramento, CA 95814
phone: 916-445-3685
e-mail: dyparraguirre@dfg.ca.gov

**Guy Zenner** (Mississippi Flyway)
Iowa Dept. of Natural Resources
1203 North Shore Drive
Clear Lake, IA   50428
phone: 515-357-3517, ext. 23
fax: 515-357-5523
e-mail: gzenner@netins.net

# APPENDIX B: Mid-continent Mallard Models

## Model Structure

In 2002 we extensively revised the set of alternative models describing the population dynamics of mid-continent mallards (Runge et al. 2002, USFWS 2002). Collectively, the models express uncertainty (or disagreement) about whether harvest is an additive or compensatory form of mortality (Burnham et al. 1984), and whether the reproductive process is weakly or strongly density-dependent (i.e., the degree to which reproductive rates decline with increasing population size).

All population models for mid-continent mallards share a common "balance equation" to predict changes in breeding-population size as a function of annual survival and reproductive rates:

$$N_{t+1} = N_t \left( mS_{t,AM} + \left(1 - m\right)\left(S_{t,AF} + R_t\left(S_{t,JF} + S_{t,JM}\ \phi_F^{sum} / \phi_M^{sum}\right)\right)\right)$$

where:
$N$ = breeding population size,
$m$ = proportion of males in the breeding population,
$S_{AM}$, $S_{AF}$, $S_{JF}$, and $S_{JM}$ = survival rates of adult males, adult females, young females, and young males, respectively,
$R$ = reproductive rate, defined as the fall age ratio of females,
$\phi_F^{sum} / \phi_M^{sum}$ = the ratio of female ($F$) to male ($M$) summer survival, and
$t$ = year.

We assumed that $m$ and $\phi_F^{sum} / \phi_M^{sum}$ are fixed and known. We also assumed, based in part on information provided by Blohm et al. (1987), the ratio of female to male summer survival was equivalent to the ratio of annual survival rates in the absence of harvest. Based on this assumption, we estimated $\phi_F^{sum} / \phi_M^{sum} = 0.897$. To estimate $m$ we expressed the balance equation in matrix form:

$$\begin{bmatrix} N_{t+1,AM} \\ N_{t+1,AF} \end{bmatrix} = \begin{bmatrix} S_{AM} & RS_{JM}\ \phi_F^{sum} / \phi_M^{sum} \\ 0 & S_{AF} + RS_{JF} \end{bmatrix} \begin{bmatrix} N_{t,AM} \\ N_{t,AF} \end{bmatrix}$$

and substituted the constant ratio of summer survival and means of estimated survival and reproductive rates. The right eigenvector of the transition matrix is the stable sex structure that the breeding population eventually would attain with these constant demographic rates. This eigenvector yielded an estimate of $m = 0.5246$.

Using estimates of annual survival and reproductive rates, the balance equation for mid-continent mallards over-predicted observed population sizes by 10.8% on average. The source of the bias is unknown, so we modified the balance equation to eliminate the bias by adjusting both survival and reproductive rates:

$$N_{t+1} = \gamma_S N_t \left( mS_{t,AM} + \left(1 - m\right)\left(S_{t,AF} + \gamma_R R_t\left(S_{t,JF} + S_{t,JM}\ \phi_F^{sum} / \phi_M^{sum}\right)\right)\right)$$

where $\gamma$ denotes the bias-correction factors for survival ($S$) and reproduction ($R$). We used a least squares approach to estimate $\gamma_S = 0.9479$ and $\gamma_R = 0.8620$.

## Survival Process

We considered two alternative hypotheses for the relationship between annual survival and harvest rates. For both models, we assumed that survival in the absence of harvest was the same for adults and young of the same sex. In the model where harvest mortality is additive to natural mortality:

$$S_{t,sex,age} = s_{0,sex}^{A}\left(1 - K_{t,sex,age}\right)$$

and in the model where changes in natural mortality compensate for harvest losses (up to some threshold):

$$S_{t,sex,age} = \begin{cases} s_{0,sex}^{C} & \text{if } K_{t,sex,age} \leq 1 - s_{0,sex}^{C} \\ 1 - K_{t,sex,age} & \text{if } K_{t,sex,age} > 1 - s_{0,sex}^{C} \end{cases}$$

where $s_0$ = survival in the absence of harvest under the additive ($A$) or compensatory ($C$) model, and $K$ = harvest rate adjusted for crippling loss (20%, Anderson and Burnham 1976). We averaged estimates of $s_0$ across banding reference areas by weighting by breeding-population size. For the additive model, $s_0 = 0.7896$ and $0.6886$ for males and females, respectively. For the compensatory model, $s_0 = 0.6467$ and $0.5965$ for males and females, respectively. These estimates may seem counterintuitive because survival in the absence of harvest should be the same for both models. However, estimating a common (but still sex-specific) $s_0$ for both models leads to alternative models that do not fit available band-recovery data equally well. More importantly, it suggests that the greatest uncertainty about survival rates is when harvest rate is within the realm of experience. By allowing $s_0$ to differ between additive and compensatory models, we acknowledge that the greatest uncertainty about survival rate is its value in the absence of harvest (i.e., where we have no experience).

## Reproductive Process

Annual reproductive rates were estimated from age ratios in the harvest of females, corrected using a constant estimate of differential vulnerability. Predictor variables were the number of ponds in May in Prairie Canada ($P$, in millions) and the size of the breeding population ($N$, in millions). We estimated the best-fitting linear model, and then calculated the 80% confidence ellipsoid for all model parameters. We chose the two points on this ellipsoid with the largest and smallest values for the effect of breeding-population size, and generated a weakly density-dependent model:

$$R_t = 0.7166 + 0.1083P_t - 0.0373N_t$$

and a strongly density-dependent model:

$$R_t = 1.1390 + 0.1376P_t - 0.1131N_t$$

## Pond Dynamics

We modeled annual variation in Canadian pond numbers as a first-order autoregressive process. The estimated model was:

$$P_{t+1} = 2.2127 + 0.3420P_t + \varepsilon_t$$

where ponds are in millions and $\varepsilon_t$ is normally distributed with mean = 0 and variance = 1.2567.

## Variance of Prediction Errors

Using the balance equation and sub-models described above, predictions of breeding-population size in year $t+1$ depend only on specification of population size, pond numbers, and harvest rate in year $t$. For the period in which comparisons were possible, we compared these predictions with observed population sizes.

We estimated the prediction-error variance by setting:

$$e_t = \ln\left(N_t^{obs}\right) - \ln\left(N_t^{pre}\right)$$

$$\text{then assuming} \quad e_t \sim N\left(0, \sigma^2\right)$$

$$\text{and estimating} \quad \hat{\sigma}^2 = \sum_t \left[\ln\left(N_t^{obs}\right) - \ln\left(N_t^{pre}\right)\right]^2 \Big/ (n-1)$$

where *obs* and *pre* are observed and predicted population sizes (in millions), respectively, and $n$ = the number of years being compared. We were concerned about a variance estimate that was too small, either by chance or because the number of years in which comparisons were possible was small. Therefore, we calculated the upper 80% confidence limit for $\sigma^2$ based on a Chi-squared distribution for each combination of the alternative survival and reproductive sub-models, and then averaged them. The final estimate of $\sigma^2$ was 0.0243, equivalent to a coefficient of variation of about 17%.

## Model Implications

The set of alternative population models suggests that carrying capacity (average population size in the absence of harvest) for an average number of Canadian ponds is somewhere between about 6 and 16 million mallards. The population model with additive hunting mortality and weakly density-dependent recruitment (SaRw) leads to the most conservative harvest strategy, whereas the model with compensatory hunting mortality and strongly density-dependent recruitment (ScRs) leads to the most liberal strategy. The other two models (SaRs and ScRw) lead to strategies that are intermediate between these extremes. Under the models with compensatory hunting mortality (ScRs and ScRw), the optimal strategy is to have a liberal regulation regardless of population size or number of ponds because at harvest rates achieved under the liberal alternative, harvest has no effect on population size. Under the strongly density-dependent model (ScRs), the density-dependence regulates the population and keeps it within narrow bounds. Under the weakly density-dependent model (ScRw), the density-dependence does not exert as strong a regulatory effect, and the population size fluctuates more.

## Model Weights

Model weights are calculated as Bayesian probabilities, reflecting the relative ability of the individual alternative models to predict observed changes in population size. The Bayesian probability for each model is a function of the model's previous (or prior) weight and the likelihood of the observed population size under that model. We used Bayes' theorem to calculate model weights from a comparison of predicted and observed population sizes for the years 1996-2004, starting with equal model weights in 1995. For the purposes of updating, we predicted breeding-population size in the traditional survey area in year $t + 1$, from breeding-population size, Canadian ponds, and harvest rates in year $t$.

36

# Inclusion of Mallards in the Great Lakes Region

Model development originally did not include mallards breeding in the states of Wisconsin, Minnesota, and Michigan, primarily because full data sets were not available from these areas to permit the necessary analysis. However, mallards in the Great Lakes region have been included in the mid-continent mallard AHM protocol since 1997 by assuming that population dynamics for these mallards are similar to those in the traditional survey area. Based on that assumption, predictions of breeding population size are scaled to reflect inclusion of mallards in the Great Lakes region. From 1992 through 2007, when population estimates were available for all three states, the average proportion of the total mid-continent mallard population that was in the Great Lakes region was 0.1099 (SD = 0.0207). We assumed a normal distribution with these parameter values to make the conversion between the traditional survey area and total breeding-population size.

# APPENDIX C: Eastern Mallard Models

## Model Structure

We also revised the population models for eastern mallards in 2002 (Johnson et al. 2002*a*, USFWS 2002). The current set of six models: (1) relies solely on federal and state waterfowl surveys (rather than the Breeding Bird Survey) to estimate abundance; (2) allows for the possibility of a positive bias in estimates of survival or reproductive rates; (3) incorporates competing hypotheses of strongly and weakly density-dependent reproduction; and (4) assumes that hunting mortality is additive to other sources of mortality.

As with mid-continent mallards, all population models for eastern mallards share a common balance equation to predict changes in breeding-population size as a function of annual survival and reproductive rates:

$$N_{t+1} = N_t \cdot \left( \left( p \cdot S_t^{am} \right) + \left( (1-p) \cdot S_t^{af} \right) + \left( p \cdot \left( A_t^m / d \right) \cdot S_t^{ym} \right) + \left( p \cdot \left( A_t^m / d \right) \cdot \psi \cdot S_t^{yf} \right) \right)$$

where:
$N$ = breeding-population size,
$p$ = proportion of males in the breeding population,
$S^{am}$, $S^{af}$, $S^{ym}$, and $S^{yf}$ = survival rates of adult males, adult females, young males, and young females, respectively,
$A^m$ = ratio of young males to adult males in the harvest,
$d$ = ratio of young male to adult male direct recovery rates,
$\psi$ = the ratio of male to female summer survival, and $t$ = year.

In this balance equation, we assume that $p$, $d$, and $\psi$ are fixed and known. The parameter $\psi$ is necessary to account for the difference in anniversary date between the breeding-population survey (May) and the survival and reproductive rate estimates (August). This model also assumes that the sex ratio of fledged young is 1:1; hence $A^m/d$ appears twice in the balance equation. We estimated $d = 1.043$ as the median ratio of young:adult male band-recovery rates in those states from which wing receipts were obtained. We estimated $\psi = 1.216$ by regressing through the origin estimates of male survival against female survival in the absence of harvest, assuming that differences in natural mortality between males and females occur principally in summer. To estimate $p$, we used a population projection matrix of the form:

$$\begin{bmatrix} M_{t+1} \\ F_{t+1} \end{bmatrix} = \begin{bmatrix} S^{am} + \left( A^m / d \right) \cdot S^{ym} & 0 \\ \left( A^m / d \right) \cdot \psi \cdot S^{yf} & S^{af} \end{bmatrix} \cdot \begin{bmatrix} M_t \\ F_t \end{bmatrix}$$

where $M$ and $F$ are the relative number of males and females in the breeding populations, respectively. To parameterize the projection matrix we used average annual survival rate and age ratio estimates, and the estimates of $d$ and $\psi$ provided above. The right eigenvector of the projection matrix is the stable proportion of males and females the breeding population eventually would attain in the face of constant demographic rates. This eigenvector yielded an estimate of $p = 0.544$.

We also attempted to determine whether estimates of survival and reproductive rates were unbiased. We relied on the balance equation provided above, except that we included additional parameters to correct for any bias that might exist. Because we were unsure of the source(s) of potential bias, we alternatively assumed that any bias resided solely in survival rates:

$$N_{t+1} = N_t \cdot \Omega \cdot \left( \left( p \cdot S_t^{am} \right) + \left( (1-p) \cdot S_t^{af} \right) + \left( p \cdot \left( A_t^m / d \right) \cdot S_t^{ym} \right) + \left( p \cdot \left( A_t^m / d \right) \cdot \psi \cdot S_t^{yf} \right) \right)$$

(where $\Omega$ is the bias-correction factor for survival rates), or solely in reproductive rates:

$$N_{t+1} = N_t \cdot \left( \left( p \cdot S_t^{am} \right) + \left( (1-p) \cdot S_t^{af} \right) + \left( p \cdot \alpha \cdot \left( A_t^m / d \right) \cdot S_t^{ym} \right) + \left( p \cdot \alpha \cdot \left( A_t^m / d \right) \cdot \psi \cdot S_t^{yf} \right) \right)$$

(where $\alpha$ is the bias-correction factor for reproductive rates). We estimated $\Omega$ and $\alpha$ by determining the values of these parameters that minimized the sum of squared differences between observed and predicted population sizes. Based on this analysis, $\Omega = 0.836$ and $\alpha = 0.701$, suggesting a positive bias in survival or reproductive rates. However, because of the limited number of years available for comparing observed and predicted population sizes, we also retained the balance equation that assumes estimates of survival and reproductive rates are unbiased.

## Survival Process

For purposes of AHM, annual survival rates must be predicted based on the specification of regulation-specific harvest rates (and perhaps on other uncontrolled factors). Annual survival for each age ($i$) and sex ($j$) class under a given regulatory alternative is:

$$S_t^{i,j} = \overline{\theta}^{\,j} \cdot \left( 1 - \frac{\left( h_t^{am} \cdot v^{i,j} \right)}{(1-c)} \right)$$

where:

$S$ = annual survival,

$\overline{\theta}^{\,j}$ = mean survival from natural causes,

$h^{am}$ = harvest rate of adult males, and

$v$ = harvest vulnerability relative to adult males,

$c$ = rate of crippling (unretrieved harvest).

This model assumes that annual variation in survival is due solely to variation in harvest rates, that relative harvest vulnerability of the different age-sex classes is fixed and known, and that survival from natural causes is fixed at its sample mean. We estimated $\overline{\theta}^{\,j} = 0.7307$ and $0.5950$ for males and females, respectively.

## Reproductive process

As with survival, annual reproductive rates must be predicted in advance of setting regulations. We relied on the apparent relationship between breeding-population size and reproductive rates:

$$R_t = a \cdot \exp(b \cdot N_t)$$

where $R_t$ is the reproductive rate (i.e., $A_t^m / d$), $N_t$ is breeding-population size in millions, and $a$ and $b$ are model parameters. The least-squares parameter estimates were $a = 2.508$ and $b = -0.875$. Because of both the importance and uncertainty of the relationship between population size and reproduction, we specified two alternative models in which the slope ($b$) was fixed at the least-squares estimate $\pm$ one standard error, and in which the intercepts ($a$) were subsequently re-estimated. This provided alternative hypotheses of strongly density-dependent ($a = 4.154$, $b = -1.377$) and weakly density-dependent reproduction ($a = 1.518$, $b = -0.373$).

## Variance of Prediction Errors

Using the balance equations and sub-models provided above, predictions of breeding-population size in year $t+1$ depend only on the specification of a regulatory alternative and on an estimate of population size in year $t$. For the period in which comparisons were possible (1991-96), we were interested in how well these predictions corresponded with observed population sizes. In making these comparisons, we were primarily concerned with how well the bias-corrected balance equations and reproductive and survival sub-models performed. Therefore, we relied on estimates of harvest rates rather than regulations as model inputs.

We estimated the prediction-error variance by setting:

$$e_t = \ln\left(N_t^{obs}\right) - \ln\left(N_t^{pre}\right)$$

then assuming $e_t \sim N\left(0, \sigma^2\right)$

and estimating $\hat{\sigma}^2 = \sum_t \left[\ln\left(N_t^{obs}\right) - \ln\left(N_t^{pre}\right)\right]^2 \Big/ n$

where $obs$ and $pre$ are observed and predicted population sizes (in millions), respectively, and $n = 6$.

Variance estimates were similar regardless of whether we assumed that the bias was in reproductive rates or in survival, or whether we assumed that reproduction was strongly or weakly density-dependent. Thus, we averaged variance estimates to provide a final estimate of $\sigma^2 = 0.006$, which is equivalent to a coefficient of variation (CV) of 8.0%. We were concerned, however, about the small number of years available for estimating this variance. Therefore, we estimated an 80% confidence interval for $\sigma^2$ based on a Chi-squared distribution and used the upper limit for $\sigma^2 = 0.018$ (i.e., $CV = 14.5\%$) to express the additional uncertainty about the magnitude of prediction errors attributable to potentially important environmental effects not expressed by the models.

## Model Implications

Model-specific regulatory strategies based on the hypothesis of weakly density-dependent reproduction are considerably more conservative than those based on the hypothesis of strongly density-dependent reproduction. The three models with weakly density-dependent reproduction suggest a carrying capacity (i.e., average population size in the absence of harvest) >2.0 million mallards, and prescribe extremely restrictive regulations for population size <1.0 million. The three models with strongly density-dependent reproduction suggest a carrying capacity of about 1.5 million mallards, and prescribe liberal regulations for population sizes >300 thousand. Optimal regulatory strategies are relatively insensitive to whether models include a bias correction or not. All model-specific regulatory strategies are "knife-edged," meaning that large differences in the optimal regulatory choice can be precipitated by only small changes in breeding-population size. This result is at least partially due to the small differences in predicted harvest rates among the current regulatory alternatives (see the section on Regulatory Alternatives later in this report).

## Model Weights

We used Bayes' theorem to calculate model weights from a comparison of predicted and observed population sizes for the years 1996-2006. We calculated weights for the alternative models based on an assumption of equal model weights in 1996 (the last year data was used to develop most model components) and on estimates of year-specific harvest rates (Appendix D).

# APPENDIX D: Modeling Mallard Harvest Rates

We modeled harvest rates of mid-continent mallards within a Bayesian hierarchical framework. We developed a set of models to predict harvest rates under each regulatory alternative as a function of the harvest rates observed under the liberal alternative, using historical information relating harvest rates to various regulatory alternatives. We modeled the probability of regulation-specific harvest rates ($h$) based on normal distributions with the following parameterizations:

Closed: $\quad p(h_C) \sim N(\mu_C, v_C^2)$

Restrictive: $\quad p(h_R) \sim N(\gamma_R \mu_L, v_R^2)$

Moderate: $\quad p(h_M) \sim N(\gamma_M \mu_L + \delta_f, v_M^2)$

Liberal: $\quad p(h_L) \sim N(\mu_L + \delta_f, v_L^2)$

For the restrictive and moderate alternatives we introduced the parameter $\gamma$ to represent the relative difference between the harvest rate observed under the liberal alternative and the moderate or restrictive alternatives. Based on this parameterization, we are making use of the information that has been gained (under the liberal alternative) and are modeling harvest rates for the restrictive and moderate alternatives as a function of the mean harvest rate observed under the liberal alternative. For the harvest-rate distributions assumed under the restrictive and moderate regulatory packages, we specified that $\gamma_R$ and $\gamma_M$ are equal to the prior estimates of the predicted mean harvest rates under the restrictive and moderate alternatives divided by the prior estimates of the predicted mean harvest rates observed under the liberal alternative. Thus, these parameters act to scale the mean of the restrictive and moderate distributions in relation to the mean harvest rate observed under the liberal regulatory alternative. We also considered the marginal effect of framework-date extensions under the moderate and liberal alternatives by including the parameter $\delta_f$.

In order to update the probability distributions of harvest rates realized under each regulatory alternative, we first needed to specify a prior probability distribution for each of the model parameters. These distributions represent prior beliefs regarding the relationship between each regulatory alternative and the expected harvest rates. We used a normal distribution to represent the mean and a scaled inverse-chi-square distribution to represent the variance of the normal distribution of the likelihood. For the mean ($\mu$) of each harvest-rate distribution associated with each regulatory alternative, we use the predicted mean harvest rates provided in USFWS (2000$a$:13-14), assuming uniformity of regulatory prescriptions across flyways. We set prior values of each standard deviation ($v$) equal to 20% of the mean (CV = 0.2) based on an analysis by Johnson et al. (1997). We then specified the following prior distributions and parameter values under each regulatory package:

*Closed (in U.S. only):*

$$p(\mu_C) \sim N(0.0088, \frac{0.0018^2}{6})$$

$$p(v_C^2) \sim Scaled\ Inv\ \text{-}\ \chi^2(6, 0.0018^2)$$

These closed-season parameter values are based on observed harvest rates in Canada during the 1988-93 seasons, which was a period of restrictive regulations in both Canada and the United States.

For the restrictive and moderate alternatives, we specified that the standard error of the normal distribution of the scaling parameter is based on a coefficient of variation for the mean equal to 0.3. The scale parameter of the inverse-chi-square distribution was set equal to the standard deviation of the harvest rate mean under the restrictive and moderate regulation alternatives (i.e., CV = 0.2).

*Restrictive:*

$$p(\gamma_R) \sim N(0.51, \frac{0.15^2}{6})$$

$$p(v_R^2) \sim \text{Scaled Inv} - \chi^2(6, 0.0133^2)$$

*Moderate:*

$$p(\gamma_M) \sim N(0.85, \frac{0.26^2}{6})$$

$$p(v_M^2) \sim \text{Scaled Inv} - \chi^2(6, 0.0223^2)$$

*Liberal:*

$$p(\mu_L) \sim N(0.1305, \frac{0.0261^2}{6})$$

$$p(v_L^2) \sim \text{Scaled Inv} - \chi^2(6, 0.0261^2)$$

The prior distribution for the marginal effect of the framework-date extension was specified as:

$$p(\delta_f) \sim N(0.02, 0.01^2)$$

The prior distributions were multiplied by the likelihood functions based on the last seven years of data under liberal regulations, and the resulting posterior distributions were evaluated with Markov Chain Monte Carlo simulation. Posterior estimates of model parameters and of annual harvest rates are provided in the following table:

| Parameter | Estimate | SD | Parameter | Estimate | SD |
|-----------|----------|--------|-----------|----------|--------|
| $\mu_C$ | 0.0088 | 0.0022 | $h_{1998}$ | 0.1098 | 0.0113 |
| $v_C$ | 0.0019 | 0.0005 | $h_{1999}$ | 0.1002 | 0.0076 |
| $\gamma_R$ | 0.5090 | 0.0617 | $h_{2000}$ | 0.1252 | 0.0099 |
| $v_R$ | 0.0129 | 0.0033 | $h_{2001}$ | 0.1068 | 0.0112 |
| $\gamma_M$ | 0.8530 | 0.1062 | $h_{2002}$ | 0.1145 | 0.0057 |
| $v_M$ | 0.0216 | 0.0055 | $h_{2003}$ | 0.1100 | 0.0064 |
| $\mu_L$ | 0.1139 | 0.0070 | $h_{2004}$ | 0.11188 | 0.0098 |
| $v_L$ | 0.0205 | 0.0055 | $h_{2005}$ | 0.1158 | 0.0081 |
| $\delta_f$ | 0.0087 | 0.0079 | $h_{2006}$ | 0.1061 | 0.0073 |

We modeled harvest rates of eastern mallards using the same parameterizations as those for mid-continent mallards:

Closed: $\quad p(h_C) \sim N(\mu_C, v_C^2)$

Restrictive: $\quad p(h_R) \sim N(\gamma_R \mu_L, v_R^2)$

Moderate: $\quad p(h_M) \sim N(\gamma_M \mu_L + \delta_f, v_M^2)$

Liberal: $\quad p(h_L) \sim N(\mu_L + \delta_f, v_L^2)$

We set prior values of each standard deviation (v) equal to 30% of the mean (CV = 0.3) to account for additional variation due to changes in regulations in the other Flyways and their unpredictable effects on the harvest rates of eastern mallards. We then specified the following prior distribution and parameter values for the liberal regulatory alternative:

***Liberal:***

$$p(\mu_L) \sim N(0.1771, \frac{0.0531^2}{6})$$

$$p(v_L^2) \sim Scaled\ Inv\text{-}\chi^2(6, 0.0531^2)$$

***Moderate:***

$$p(\gamma_M) \sim N(0.92, \frac{0.28^2}{6})$$

$$p(v_M^2) \sim Scaled\ Inv\text{-}\chi^2(6, 0.0488^2)$$

***Restrictive:***

$$p(\gamma_R) \sim N(0.76, \frac{0.28^2}{6})$$

$$p(v_R^2) \sim Scaled\ Inv\text{-}\chi^2(6, 0.0406^2)$$

***Closed (in U.S. only):***

$$p(\mu_C) \sim N(0.0800, \frac{0.0240^2}{6})$$

$$p(v_C^2) \sim Scaled\ Inv\text{-}\chi^2(6, 0.0240^2)$$

A previous analysis suggested that the effect of the framework-date extension on eastern mallards would be of lower magnitude and more variable than on mid-continent mallards (USFWS 2000). Therefore, we specified the following prior distribution for the marginal effect of the framework-date extension for eastern mallards as:

$$p(\delta_f) \sim N(0.01, 0.01^2)$$

The prior distributions were multiplied by the likelihood functions based on the last four years of data under liberal regulations, and the resulting posterior distributions were evaluated with Markov Chain Monte Carlo simulation. Posterior estimates of model parameters and of annual harvest rates are provided in the following table:

| Parameter | Estimate | SD | Parameter | Estimate | SD |
|-----------|----------|--------|-----------|----------|--------|
| $\mu_C$ | 0.0798 | 0.0262 | $h_{2002}$ | 0.1627 | 0.0129 |
| $v_C$ | 0.0233 | 0.0059 | $h_{2003}$ | 0.1462 | 0.0104 |
| $\gamma_R$ | 0.7642 | 0.1144 | $h_{2004}$ | 0.1364 | 0.0114 |
| $v_R$ | 0.0395 | 0.0104 | $h_{2005}$ | 0.1311 | 0.0120 |
| $\gamma_M$ | 0.9187 | 0.1148 | $h_{2006}$ | 0.1048 | 0.0134 |
| $v_M$ | 0.0474 | 0.0121 | | | |
| $\mu_L$ | 0.1532 | 0.0166 | | | |
| $v_L$ | 0.0459 | 0.0099 | | | |
| $\delta_f$ | 0.0046 | 0.0096 | | | |

www.ingramcontent.com/pod-product-compliance
Lightning Source LLC
Chambersburg PA
CBHW080621290526
45790CB00007B/2865